MW00817025

The Mindset of a Dyslexic Ǝntrepreneur

Dr. Don Steele

with
Lawrence L. Allen

I dedicate this book to my father's memory,
Marine Lieutenant Stanley F. Holman,
DDS, whose life lived was my example
and who believed in me.
And he was a gentleman's gentleman.

— Scott L. Holman

I would like to acknowledge all the people who contributed their insights, anecdotes, comments, and quotes to this book: Brad Canale, Greg Messenger, Jene Quirin, Bill Schutte, and Rich Studley. A special thanks to Larry Elliott, Elizabeth Wahlstrom, and Jerry Linenger for each contributing a chapter, and Thomas Zurbuchen for an insightful and touching Foreword. And, of course, a heartfelt thanks to my lovely and charming wife, Martine, for supporting the writing of this book. Finally, Dr. Don Steele: thank you for convincing me that the world needed to hear my story.

— Scott L. Holman

Contents

Foreword
Thomas H. Zurbuchen

I met Scott Holman in 2014 when he was appointed trustee to Northern Michigan University, his alma mater. It was his second term on the board. On the surface, we could not be any more different. I was an academic born in Switzerland and an immigrant to the United States, working as a professor elsewhere in Michigan who visited Michigan's Upper Peninsula for the first time when the governor nominated me as trustee. He was a businessman with deep roots in the UP, who was an NMU alumnus from a time when I was approximately one year old, and a man who could not walk down any road in Marquette without being recognized and greeted.

It only took me one or two meetings before I started to get to know Scott and the very stories that make this book so worth reading. Scott is a dear friend to me, one that I would trust with my life, and one that has made the UP one of my favorite places on Earth.

Fall in Michigan's Upper Peninsula

When I think of Scott Holman, I think first of the origin story that gave this book its title. Scott cannot be understood without learning about his dyslexia. Overlooked for years, losing many opportunities, called stupid by many—even teachers—and almost believing the name-callers, Scott came to Northern Michigan University where his professors and mentors recognized his dyslexia and helped turn things around. What comes next is a story of perseverance and hard work—Michigan Upper Peninsula SISU-style—that allowed him to prove a doubting world wrong with a life well lived and much-deserved hard-won success.

Like Charles Schwab, Ikea founder Ingvar Kamprad, Albert Einstein, and Richard Branson, having a learning difference like dyslexia may be a hindrance in school, but is a superpower that creates new ways of looking at the world, and is an enabler for entrepreneurial thinking and action. Thinking differently creates different, and often novel, outcomes. Look at Scott's business successes that are well-described in this book. Above all, consider Bay Cast Incorporated and Bay Cast Technologies, businesses reimagined Holman-style. I built one of the leading entrepreneurial education programs in the US and had the pleasure and honor to get to know so many entrepreneurial minds, and I can say that, without doubt, Scott is one of the best. I can also say that Scott is among many fellow dyslexics in the community of entrepreneurs I got to know. It is not just his companies where his dyslexia created magic; it is how he wired up his piece of paradise near King Lake and the lighthouse he rescued on Granite Island with advanced communication technologies that made the jaw drop. Entrepreneurship is what bursts out of Scott's mind every time he gets to know a new program, and entrepreneurial wisdom is what you learn if you take time to listen.

Scott had many of his successes downstate, around the US, and around the world, without ever moving one iota away from his UP heritage. You cannot know Scott without knowing the UP. He will make you come visit him and his wonderful restaurant. He will tell you stories of his childhood, his diving, and his family; how he met the love of his life, Martine; and how he bought an island in Lake Superior. Those are the stories of this book.

The first pasty of my life was eaten on his rocky island, together with my son, who was also invited to visit it through choppy waters. I still remember how Scott admired my son for managing to eat not one but two pasties and loved them. "That is quite an achievement," he said. I spent some of our family's favorite vacations in the UP, often as Scott's guest or sometimes at locations based on his recommendation. We hiked and experienced sunsets in the UP wilderness, sunsets that somehow cannot be captured with a camera because they lose the depth and magnitude of the live experience, with all the sounds of birds and the quiet and sudden splashing of fish in the water breaking the deep silence. No cars. And when the sun is down, right next to the US flag that flies in every one of Scott's places, the dark skies open, revealing the magnificent universe to those who take time to watch. Scott is a true naturalist, not one that puts stickers on cars and screams at others about his opinions, but one that quietly preserves nature and gives homes to animals that I had only met in zoos or read about in books. Scott is a Yooper based on his roots, but also based on who he is and where his heart is.

During every NMU Board meeting, there were legal briefings reminding us to be careful not to congregate as a quorum and to be aware of where we discussed our business. Yes, the community was deeply aware and interested in our work. I learned that very quickly when the university president asked me politely after a couple of board meetings to please visit not just one but also the other local brewery. The owner of that business had complained that I only frequented his competitor.

Scott always understood the UP and Marquette communities and thus he reserved a suite at the Landmark, his favorite hotel due to its history, and invited fellow board members for drinks and snacks. This is where we got to know each other and became friends. Some of us were appointed by the same governor that Scott was; others were appointed by the previous governor from a different party. All of that did not matter; we were just friends who cared for one another and tried hard to get to know each other so we could do the best job possible to serve Northern Michigan University, the university that gave Scott Holman a chance that he needed.

Scott Holman lives a life as an entrepreneur, a family man, a friend, and a Yooper throughout, who, each day of his life, continues to prove wrong those who were too short-sighted and stupid to see the man with the dyslexic brain who was going to become one of the biggest successes around!

—Thomas H. Zurbuchen
   NMU Trustee, 2013–2016
   NMU Honorary Doctorate, 2022
   NASA Head of Science, 2016–2022

Note From the Author
Dr. Don Steele

In the course of my career, I've had the privilege of meeting, working with, and befriending top-level performers in music, sports, and business. This includes having the honor of playing music together with the likes of Willie Nelson and Tammy Wynette. What I've learned over my eighty-two years is that the same talent, determination, and moxie that make the famous successful can be found in people who lead more ordinary lives—whose no less miraculous achievements aren't obscured by the white-hot spotlight of fame. This book is about just such a person. A man who led an extraordinary life, but who is only known to his loving family and those whose lives he touched personally or through his philanthropy.

My co-author, Lawrence Allen, and I interviewed Scott's friends, family members, business associates, and others personally in an effort to ground this narrative work in supportive evidence. While telling Scott's story, we used three psychological and sociological tools to provide a framework for understanding the mindset of this remarkable entrepreneur.

First, we employed Morris Massey's value analysis theory. During the 1980s, Massey, a marketing professor and sociologist, began promoting his value analysis theory, which is summed up in the statement, "You are what you were when you were value programmed." He broke his value-based view of psychological development into three stages: the Imprint Period, the Modeling Period, and the Socialization Period.

The Imprint years cover the formative years: birth through the age of seven. It is a period where we freely absorb the world around us and accept it as reality and the truth. During this period, we develop our fundamental understanding of good and bad, right and wrong.

The Modeling Period covers the ages between eight and thirteen. During this span of years, we tend to copy people—most often parents and siblings, but this also includes people like preachers, teachers, and coaches.

The Socialization Period occurs between the ages of thirteen and twenty-one. It is a time in our lives when we start to become strongly influenced by our peers. It is when we become young adults, individuals, and begin to look for our chosen community outside our family.

Next, we mapped Scott's behaviors, efforts, challenges, and achievements against Martin Seligman's PERMA Model of well-being that identifies five characteristics of a flourishing individual:

P: Positive emotions refers to one's willingness and ability to express and inspire positive emotions with those they are in contact with. When we experience positive emotions (like hope, trust, pride, awe, or satisfaction), this opens up various centers of the brain that are less accessible or even inaccessible when we are experiencing negative emotions. Developing gratitude is key.

E: Engagement and flow includes the loss of self-consciousness, and complete absorption in an activity. Simply stated, it is living in the present moment and focusing entirely on what it is you are doing.

R: Relationships matter. Some research suggests that keeping in touch with people who matter to you relates to reduced chances of inflammation (which is, as we know, the basis of all diseases). Be proactive in keeping in touch with people who matter to you.

M: Meaning, purpose, and direction. Some people talk about dedicating themselves to something greater than themselves as providing them with a sense of meaning. For others, having a general direction toward growth or greater job satisfaction is more than enough. A great place to start is reflecting on your personal values.

A: Accomplishments. This pillar of Seligman's growth mindset model focuses on how to gain mastery and why it matters. Achievements and accomplishments up our well-being and confidence. According to Seligman's research, achieving intrinsic goals, like those relating to personal growth, leads to larger gains in well-being than extrinsic goals, such as money or fame.

Finally, we incorporated the cognitive psychology and neuroscience coaching information with a focus on Scott's thought processes—more specifically, the controlled internal dialogue that guided Scott through his personal and professional life. As you read through the chapters of this book, you will see various manifestations of it in Scott, revealing his personal "It Factor" behind his success.

Thank you, Scott, for your years of personal friendship and generosity, and for entrusting me to tell your story for the benefit of your posterity and all who learn from your life experience.

—Don Steele, PhD, co-author of *The Mindset of a Dyslexic Entrepreneur*

Prologue

Through the frosted edges of the window of his six-passenger Rockwell Twin Commander airplane, Scott Holman watched the southern shoreline of his beloved Michigan Upper Peninsula slowly peel back like a curtain, revealing the ice blue waters of northern Lake Michigan. There were whitecaps on the lake that day, typical for mid-December in Northern Michigan.

It was a majestic view that incited daydreams. And although Scott had once been admonished as being a daydreamer, he couldn't prevent decades of memories from his life commuting between Michigan's  upper and lower peninsulas to bubble up into his consciousness: memories such as pangs of anticipation while opening up his 300cc motorcycle full throttle on lonely stretches of US-41 between the cities of Marquette and Michigamme to be on time for his French damsel-in-waiting. The echo of the applause of Russian proto-business leaders after making his "Running a Business in an Entrepreneurial Environment" speech in a Kremlin conference room in Moscow, Russia. Recognizing the panic in the eyes of a scuba student and calmly helping them to the surface of Lake Superior. The report of firearms from nearby rooftops while marching in formation with his National Guard unit, bayonets affixed, on Little Mack Avenue during the '67 Detroit riots. The cheers of Bay City Foundry employees after learning they'd won the contract for NASA's Space Shuttle crawler-transporter tread shoes, while he worked out how they were going to deliver them on time and on budget. The harrowing cold, choppy, and windswept twelve-mile winter boat ride back to shore after he and a buddy had made some equipment fixes at the Granite Island lighthouse that he'd rescued from destruction from the elements and neglect—on the very same Lake *Gitche Gumee* that Gordon Lightfoot sang of, with "Superior . . . never gives up her dead" niggling in the back of his mind. The warm embrace of the tropical waters of the Caribbean as he and his dive party drifted past gargantuan waving fan corals. The expressions of gratitude and the enthusiastic handshakes of the Michigamme, Michigan, residents during the ribbon cutting at the Mt. Shasta Restaurant, newly renovated and opened for business by Scott, adding another summer attraction that would ensure more tourist revenue for the community. And of course the births of his three sons and nine grandchildren.

Yeah, Scott is a daydreamer alright. But is that really a bad thing?

His pilot was doing a fine job racing them downstate to the Lansing, Michigan, airport to be in time for his granddaughter's graduation ceremony. His schedule was tight that day because an hour or so earlier, Scott was on stage at the 2023 commencement ceremony at his alma mater, Northern Michigan University (NMU), in its Superior Dome, receiving his honorary doctoral degree in business from NMU President Brock Tessman. Scott received his diploma with gratitude, a handshake, and these words: "This means so much to me, more than you will ever know." And he meant it.

Scott Holman receiving his honorary doctorate from NMU

The award ceremony was the ultimate victory over a life-long battle with a learning disability that wasn't understood or accommodated when Scott attended school. From kindergarten through college, Scott had to bootstrap himself with self-learned workarounds to overcome his learning disability in ways that ultimately resulted in his earning dual bachelor's degrees in biology and business from NMU. His education—intellectually demanding, often emotionally traumatizing, and statistically improbable—culminated in receiving his doctorate at age eighty-two, which was indeed more meaningful to Scott than most other people would know or appreciate.

Earlier that year, Scott was looking out through another airplane window, this one steamed at the edges from tropical humidity. He was contemplating another battle, this one for his life. He was perturbed about having to fly to Miami from a Cayman Islands scuba diving trip to receive a $20,000-per-infusion treatment for myasthenia gravis, something his health insurance wouldn't cover unless it was administered in the United States. But the treatment was literally giving him his life back, and, though inconvenient, he counted his blessings for having the opportunity to receive it.

Myasthenia gravis is an autoimmune disease that most often afflicts men after the age of sixty. It occurs when an overactive immune system destroys muscle receptor sites for neurotransmitters, leading to debilitating muscle weakness. It can affect speech, vision, and other bodily functions, including swallowing. In 2009 Scott's left eyelid began closing at inappropriate times and he went to an optometrist who correctly diagnosed his condition as not being an eye problem but a symptom of something else—likely neurological. The ophthalmologist referred him to Dr. Kaufman, a specialist in diagnosing diseases of the eye at Michigan State University's medical school. A CT scan was done, among other tests, leading to the diagnosis that Scott's immune system was attacking his nerve endings: he was suffering from ocular myasthenia gravis. With that diagnosis, he went to specialists at the University of Michigan medical center where he was prescribed medication that had little effect.

In 2016 Scott got food poisoning and was prescribed an antibiotic, which unfortunately was contraindicated for myasthenia gravis. While attending an event, his speech became garbled so severely that he thought he was having a stroke. He drove himself to the local hospital where they diagnosed him as having a ministroke. He told the emergency room personnel that he had myasthenia gravis and they checked him over again. The hospital personnel stuck with their ministroke diagnosis and were preparing to administer him stroke medication when the admitting nurse said, "You know, I have a patient just like him who has myasthenia gravis." The stroke medication was not administered, and he was referred to a neurologist who reviewed his case and diagnosed his symptoms as a negative drug interaction between the antibiotic and ocular myasthenia gravis. He was released.

The symptoms from the negative drug interaction didn't go away, they worsened. In a matter of a few weeks, Scott lost twenty-five pounds, the result of his difficulty swallowing. Forced to stay at home, Scott and Martine did their own research and determined that the Mayo Clinic was the best in the country for myasthenia gravis. He made an appointment and flew to Rochester, Minnesota. After telling the doctor his story, she said, "My goodness, hasn't anyone treated you? You are *that* close to a complete respiratory shutdown." She took immediate and aggressive action: "We're going to begin infusing you with immune globulin, which contains antibodies that strengthen your immune system response." Scott saw immediate results: "After the third day of treatment, my symptoms were gone," Scott explains. "I felt so good that Martine and I went out for a steak dinner. I received two more days of treatment, for a total of five days, but was still left with some muscle weakness in my legs."

For the past eight years, Scott had been receiving infusions of two classes of medication monthly: one is a treatment for kidney transplant patients that blocks organ rejection by inhibiting the immune system; the other is a medication that helps block diseases and infections that would otherwise occur when taking the anti-rejection medication alone. The cost is $20,000 per single infusion. Once he completed the treatment in Miami, he would turn right around and continue his Cayman Islands scuba diving trip.

AT EIGHTY-TWO, BARRING ANY ADDITIONAL MEDICAL breakthroughs, Scott realizes he will be on this treatment for the rest of his life. But that won't stop him from continuing to live as he always has: scuba diving in the Caribbean, fixing and riding snowmobiles, boating out to and from his island,

and shaking hands with customers at his Mt. Shasta restaurant and asking them how they are enjoying their meal.

Long-time friend and this book's author, Dr. Don Steele, says, "He is taking his myasthenia gravis on in the same way he takes on everything else in his life: head-on."

Chapter 1
The SISU Yooper Innovator

Scott's fellow Norther Michigan University (NMU) Board of Trustees member Thomas Zurbuchen, NASA's longest continually serving head of science (2016–2022), describes Scott as the quintessential SISU Yooper innovator. "For those who don't know, SISU is of Finnish origin." During America's Great Immigration from Europe (1880–1920), Michigan's Upper Peninsula (UP) was an important destination for Finnish immigrants.[1] "Well, SISU is the cultural trait of being hardened enough to endure hardship over a long period of time through perseverance, resilience, stick-to-itive-ness, and just plain stubbornness. The characteristics of SISU are endurance, grit, fortitude, determination, strong will, and guts. But at the same time, they are kindhearted, curious, and eager learners. Now, Yooper? Well, that's just a Michigan term for someone who was born or lives in Michigan's Upper Peninsula."

Ishpeming

Old Ish in Ishpeming, Michigan

Scott's story begins in the small Upper Peninsula town of Ishpeming [ISH-puh-ming], Michigan, fifteen miles west of Marquette, a city on the southern shores of Lake Superior. Like so many other names of places in the state of Michigan, the word *ishpeming* is an adopted Native American word: Ojibwe for "above, in the air, on high." And like so many small towns across Michigan's UP, they were born out of fur, timber, and mining rushes. In the case of Ishpeming, it was convenient surface deposits of iron ore that literally put it on the map. Explorer Philo Everett was led to a 180-foot-high, 1,000-foot-wide iron ore mound by Native American guide Madji-Gesick. And the mine and town that followed became Ishpeming. In honor of this achievement, one of the mining companies erected a monument in 1884: a statue of a majestically posed Ojibwe brave holding a bow and arrow. Of course, the roughly six-foot standing statue is made of iron, and it is painted head to toe in natural colors. Ever thoughtful, the good people of Ishpeming thought to have the monument double as a drinking fountain —three of them: one for people, one for dogs, and one for horses. The landmark statue is fondly nicknamed "Old Ish."

The town has grown since Scott was born there, now with over 6,500 year-round residents. It retains its outdoorsman ethic, and both winter and summer sports are central to life there. This includes some of national fame: the National Ski Association was founded there in 1905. So proud of its heritage, the city is home to the Cliffs Shaft Mine Museum, which preserves the Marquette Iron Range's mining history for future generations, and the streets are decorated with ore cars and other ore mining hardware that dot the city. The natural beauty of the surrounding area consists of crystal blue lakes, rivers rushing around giant rock outcroppings, and endless trees. All told, Ishpeming was fertile ground for producing strapping young men and women ready to take on the world.

Scott's heritage is primarily Cornish English. Three of his four grandparents came from Cornwall; the other, Denmark. Cornwall is located in the extreme southwest corner of Britain on the Atlantic Ocean. It is a rugged and isolated piece of coastal land and its people are independent-minded. Folks from that part of Britain made their living fishing and mining, so their migration to Michigan's Upper Peninsula, beginning in the 1840s when their mining skills were in demand, was logical. A mining family, Scott's Cornish ancestors moved to Michigan to participate in the UP's mining boom. One of Scott's grandfathers was a mining captain and supervised mining operations all over the country and even mines in different parts of the world. He eventually settled in Michigamme, in part after being offered a permanent job there, but more importantly because Scott's grandmother insisted, "We're not moving again to any place that has snakes, spiders, or bodies buried in shallow graves." She was concerned about places like New Orleans, where graves need to be shallow owing to the high water table and the resulting propensity for the occasional casket to float out from the muddy ground when it becomes oversaturated.

So, Scott's father grew up in Michigamme, and when Scott's grandfather was assigned to build up the Ishpeming Blueberry Mine, the family made Ishpeming their permanent home. Scott's father wanted to be a dentist and took his pre-dental courses at Northern Michigan University, then earned his dental degree at Northwestern University in Chicago, beginning the family's transition to university-educated professions.

"People of the UP are a different breed," explains one fellow Yooper. "We grow up with the knowledge that opportunities come to those who are enterprising, self-reliant, and hard-working. If you have those three things you can be whatever you want in life." This is a credo that Scott embraced with a passion. Ensconced within the rugged and always staggeringly beautiful UP, Scott soldiered through a childhood filled with both joys and sorrows to take his place among some of Michigan's most prominent and well-respected business leaders. Together, Scott and his soulmate of fifty-eight years, his wife Martine, worked as a team to capture, make better, and share the opportunities that Michigan, and America of the 1960s through the 2000s, offered.

Scuba, Motorcycles, and a French Girl

While still a student at NMU, Scott started a scuba diving business out of his dorm room. He would make money taking divers out to explore area shipwrecks, diving around Granite Island, and became a distributor for U.S. Divers Company, the biggest name in the business. The U.S. Divers's salesman that he worked with later became the president of the company—a key relationship that ensured his little lake-side shop was allowed to flourish. "One of my friends' fathers ran a shipping company, and he gave me two eight-foot-by-eight-foot shipping crates that I used for storage," Scott explains. "I would put all my stock and equipment there and often sleep among the wetsuits and other equipment." His shop was called the Lake Superior Skin-Diving Company, and was located in Marquette, Michigan.

Scott Holman diving

It was at this stage of Scott's life that his serial-entrepreneurial nature began to emerge. "I've always believed in partnering with and providing value for people. I was the first person in the UP to have a scuba dive shop. I enjoyed diving, and the business not only helped pay for school, but it also supported my dive hobby." He also took the occasional commercial job, such as diving to unclog water intake screens and other underwater jobs. But recreational scuba was in its infancy, and he had to generate demand where his marketing education would come in handy. Scott explains, "I introduced people to the sport of diving. I would take people out on dives to give them a taste for it, and then they got hooked." He independently researched scuba diving papers from Scripps Research Institute in California and Woods Hole Institute in Massachusetts and compiled what he needed to teach his own classes before becoming an officially certified instructor.

Self-made scuba school
manual

Scott's self-made manual is 134 pages long and contains five classroom phases: Types of Diving, Equipment Breakdown and Operation, Diving Physics, Life-Saving and Self-Rescue Techniques, and Diving Physiology. Line-item topics included everything from pressure calculation formulas to underwater hand signals, and from how to avoid stepping on sea urchins to reading the body language of barracuda. "So when I went out to Massachusetts to receive my NAUI [National Association of Underwater Instructors] training, I brought one of my self-made manuals with me. They were impressed."

Likely one of the reasons for recreational scuba's slow off-take in the UP was the fact that the season was short, and that Lake Superior is a notoriously cold lake year-round. But Scott's enterprising nature found a solution for that, too. The northernmost lake of the North American Great Lakes, it was also naturally the coldest of the five, with the highest water temperature of the year being 65.1°F, which happened only in August. *Gitche Gumee*, as it was called in the Ojibwe Native American language, meant "great sea," and while it may have gotten a little warmer in shallow coves, at depth no one was diving without a thick wetsuit. Where others may have seen impossibility, Scott saw possibilities, and he decided to develop and sell his own line of customized wetsuits. He ordered the closed cell Neoprene sheets directly from the manufacturer, then hired a local patternmaker to provide him with standard patterns. Scott would then reproduce the pattern according to his individual customers' measurements, cut the closed cell Neoprene, and glue the pieces together. As time went on, he got more and more requests to make wetsuits for his customers, creating an additional revenue stream for his business.

While all this was going on, Scott was riding his 300cc motorcycle to and from Marquette and Ishpeming. Riding around the UP on his motorcycle, and being a double-major student at the university, a scuba instructor, and a diver master, Scott was one of the coolest guys in town. At least one French girl who had just moved to the area thought so.

Her name was Martine, and she was born and raised in Paris, France. She had a passion for travel but was stuck in a secretarial job she didn't like. Martine bought herself a ticket to the US, arriving in early 1965, at age nineteen. She planned to stay a year, then move on to Spain. Martine had made arrangements to stay with Dr. Alan Broderick and his wife, Natalie, who was a French language teacher. Scott's sister, Fae, was studying French under Natalie, and she decided to bring Martine home to meet Scott.

Scott recalls that magical encounter: "I took her home that evening by motorcycle and asked her if she'd like to have a longer motorcycle ride on the coming Saturday." And that was it: Martine arrived in Ishpeming on March 6, they met in May, and were married in September—a four-month whirlwind summer courtship that became a nearly six-decade partnership. "It's all the more remarkable when you consider that initially she didn't speak much English, and I don't speak French, but we'd both taken Spanish, so we spoke to each other in Spanish at first."

Martine wanted to go to NMU to get a degree, but as was the custom in France at the time, she finished formal school at age eighteen and then started working. She was given the option of taking her junior and senior years of high school or taking the GED test in order to get admitted to NMU. She decided to take the GED test. She passed, scoring in the ninety-sixth percentile in everything but American history. She attended NMU, graduating with highest honors and a teaching degree. She did some substitute teaching here and there, but never as a full-time teacher. Rather, she focused on raising their three sons and being grandmother to nine grand-children.

Scott and Martine Holman, Porcupine Mountain State Park

Although the family business required them to live down-state, midway up Michigan's Lower Peninsula on the shores of Lake Huron, UP living was at the heart of the Holman family. For Scott and Martine, it was in their souls.

Scott and his sons

King Lake Property

Scott's father owned a 1,200-acre hunting and fishing retreat called King Lake Wilderness Recreation Properties, about forty-five minutes west of Ishpeming. They also harvested timber there, which provided a great deal of outdoor adventure for a young man: rolling along

Young Scott on King Lake with his parents

logging roads in old trucks, cutting trails with chainsaws, and logging with horse and sleigh in the winter.

A man in love with Michigan's Upper Peninsula, Scott has fond memories of those days. Though remote and sparsely populated, life in the UP wasn't without its interesting challenges and happenings. Scott recalls, "My father was out at King Lake in his Chevy S-10 pickup and had a heart attack. Well, he drove himself to the hospital in Marquette. He even took the time to hop out of the truck and shut the gate behind him on the way out. While he was away at the hospital, when he should have been sleeping in the cabin instead of in a hospital bed, a large tree fell on the cabin right on top of his bed where he would have been sleeping. That heart attack saved his life, if you can believe it!"

Recognition for his good stewardship of the land

The cabin had to be rebuilt before the deer hunters returned for the season, and the entire family rebuilt the cabin together. Scott ended up investing in the hunting cabin, acquiring partial ownership with his father, and so his father put him in charge of King Lake. He created a master plan and began growing the land holdings from 1,200 acres to 13,000 acres, and he still owns and operates King Lake today. "It is a business. We only have about ten deer or bird hunters and fisherman on the property at a time, and only charge what we need for upkeep and to off-set costs: propane, electricity, etc. Harvesting timber under a state forest management plan is the main business."

Although Scott has been all over the world, hunting brown bear in places like Kamchatka in far eastern Russia, and diving in Australia, Venezuela, the Caribbean, and other places, his UP home has always held the most meaning for him. "I've had many wonderful experiences across the globe, but nothing compares to Michigan. Its natural resources and beauty are in a class by itself. There's nowhere in the world I'd rather be."

Chapter 2
The Imprint Years
Ages Zero to Seven

Born in 1941, just six months before the Japanese Empire's attack on the United States Naval Base at Pearl Harbor, Hawaii, the war would ensure that Scott's father would not be present for his early childhood. His father had already enlisted in the Navy when the United States got pulled into World War II later that December—he served in the Pacific theater of the war. The Marines needed dentists onboard ships, and he was transferred to Marine bootcamp so he could later serve as a shipboard dentist. A lieutenant, he was redeployed to the city of Nagasaki after the war's end in September 1945. There he would be the dentist to the GIs who were deployed in Nagasaki. Well into 1946, it was finally time for his father to come home.

"The first thing to arrive was a complete Japanese tea set that my father had sent back: exotic, delicate, beautiful, and completely unexpected. It only helped build the excitement for our father's impending return," Scott recalls. "Then he came home and, to the amazement of my two sisters and me (our third sister would be born a year later), our dad was carrying two military war souvenirs: a Japanese officer's pistol and a Samurai sword. But the important thing is that our father was finally home." Scott was five years old at the time, and his father's homecoming is still vivid in his memory seventy-eight years later.

For most children, starting school is an adventure that opens up a child's world, vastly expanding their social network while beginning a decade and a half of life as a student, when the most that people expected from them was to simply learn. But for Scott, it was the beginning of a life-long struggle with something inexplicable that would dog him throughout his K–12 education and leave indelible scars for life: it was undiagnosed dyslexia, combined with too many impatient, incompetent, and just plain nasty teachers. This noxious combination, along with a barely rudimentary under-standing of dyslexia at the time, delivered a chain of painful childhood experiences that would last Scott a lifetime. "Some of the teachers were bitter old maids," Scott volunteers. "Their taunts and insults have never left me. But they never got fired and they got away with murder, verbally abusing students. It was a bad experience with them from beginning to end."

A "word blindness" condition was discussed within medical circles in Europe in the late 1870s, and the term dyslexia was first used in the early 1880s.[1] In the United States, it wasn't until the 1970s, through things like the Education for All Handicapped Children Act of 1975, that knowledge and a basic understanding of dyslexia began to reach into classrooms. But Scott attended school decades too early to benefit from the kind of accommodations that became commonplace in schools over the past half-century—quite the opposite.

Remarkably, at age eighty-two, Scott's experiences are still fresh in his mind, starting with the very first days of school. "I had a kindergarten teacher who was just not cut out to take care of little kids. I remember her distinctly. Consequently, I tried every excuse to not go to school, including the old thermometer-near-the-hot-water-radiator trick," Scott recalls. "I told my mother that I had a fever and couldn't go to school, and then she called a doctor who would make house calls. I was left a terrible choice for a kindergartener: a pain in the butt from the doctor's needle or facing the pain-in-the-butt teacher."

Scott's first-grade teacher proved to be a temporary respite for him. She left a big impression on Scott, so much so that he fondly recalls her name: "She was Mrs. Hughes, and she was a great teacher; I can still remember her. She would read a chapter from a book to us every day in class and I loved it. She was born to teach."

But when second grade rolled around, Scott was thrust back into the undiagnosed-dyslexia purgatory that was endemic to the schools of the day. For Scott, second grade forced him into a painful moment of truth. "It was time: I was expected to learn to read. And, of course, we all had to get up in front of the class where I would have to present my deficiency for all to see. So, with book in hand, and nothing on the page making any sense, I'd freeze, not able to read or do anything." This painful memory is still with Scott to this day, three-quarters of a century later. "So the teacher starts screaming at me in front of the whole class. She grabs my shirt collar, pulls me off my feet, drags me over to the first-grade classroom, plops me down in a chair, and announces, 'This kid is too dumb for second grade. This is where he belongs.'" This horrific public display of abuse made a lasting impression on Scott's classmates, and it followed him for the rest of his K–12 experience, resulting in chronic bullying.

Chapter 3
Modeling Years
Ages Eight to Thirteen

The hits kept coming for Scott in later grades, too. "In fourth grade, we had to do something called 'picture studies.' That's when I learned to hate classic paintings. We would get a sheet of paper, with a picture of *Blue Boy* or *Mona Lisa*, or some other classic painting, and underneath the image there were lines to write on. The teacher would write a brief analysis of the image on the chalkboard, and you were supposed to write down the words onto your page. I couldn't do it, and so I was kept after class." So extreme and untreated was his dyslexia, he often spent hours after school all alone in the classroom, just sitting there, never managing to do the assignments.

Fifth grade continued the ever-escalating systematic assault on Scott's self-confidence and belief in his abilities. This time it was spelling. "In those days, classes were divided into groups: A-Group for the smart kids who regularly got As, the B-Group who got Bs, and so on. My teacher put me in the

D-Group . . . D for dummies. It was all so cruel." But when his English teacher was out for an extended illness, the substitute teacher became a bright spot in his dark world of disappointment and humiliation. "She worked with me one-on-one on spelling, so I not only passed the spelling class, but excelled: I got As and Bs. But when the regular teacher returned, she didn't accept my improved performance. She would not record the substitute teacher's A and B marks because she was convinced that I wasn't an A and B student. Even though I earned my way up through hard work and success, she still relegated me to that D-class."

Chapter 4
Socialization Years
Ages Fourteen to Twenty

All the way through high school, it was the same: one bad experience after another at the hands of people in authority over him in the education system. "There was a new, particularly cruel ritual that carried on through the remaining grades. I don't know why they did it; perhaps it was for the purpose of motivation, but when you moved to the next grade, the previous teacher wrote about you and passed their comments on to the new teacher. And if that wasn't bad enough, she would read your reviews to the new class. Me? I was labeled 'a daydreamer,' and not in the good sense."

Numbers and formulas became the next challenge for Scott. "I was okay with formulas and the processes," he explains. "I got the formulas right on tests, but I'd get the answer wrong because I'd transpose the numbers when writing them down . . . even though I knew better. It was extremely frustrating."

It wasn't until Scott was in college, enrolled in Northern Michigan University, that he finally hit his stride with education, though not without difficulty. "Once I finally discovered for myself that I wasn't stupid, that became the driving force in my life in college," Scott shares. "I discovered that my best capabilities weren't taking written exams or tests. The best part of my performance was with oral reports." Through all of the trauma, Scott knew what his shortcomings were, and they were reading and handwriting. But like many people with learning difficulties, he coped with creative workarounds.

"I could type eighty words a minute but could only handwrite ten words a minute, albeit inaccurately. So when I was getting ready for college at Northern Michigan University, I had a good high school teacher who taught Saturday writing skills classes for those of us going to college. In that class, you had to write out your assignments by hand. I kept a recorder in a briefcase to record the lecture, and I had a portable electric typewriter. When I started typing all of my assignments, I got good grades." It was a clever workaround and became a key skill that served him well in college. "Amazingly, I was accepted into NMU under President Harden's 'right to try' program [the notion that any student who wanted to pursue a college education ought to have the opportunity to seek one, irrespective of his or her past academic record]. In other words, I was accepted on probation."

But even college wasn't without its bureaucratic problems. "I routinely recorded the lecture of Dr. Gordon Gill, one of my favorite teachers, and he was very interesting, too. One day I got caught recording, which Dr. Gill mistakenly thought was against the rules, but it wasn't. Nevertheless, I got sent to the dean. The dean said to me, 'We don't know what to do, this has never happened before.' I explained why I was doing it, but the dean did not accept that. Instead, he said, 'Let's try something else,' and he had me take remedial reading classes offered at the university. It helped a little, but not that much. What followed was a speed-reading class that I immediately flunked."

During his college years (1960–1965), Scott was already beginning to think about starting his own businesses. His initial major was forestry and fisheries, and he earned enough biology credits to receive a bachelor's degree in biology. But he knew that business was going to be a big part of his life, and after receiving some advice, he went on to earn a second bachelor's in business: marketing and management. Scott had overcome huge headwinds during his academic life and won. It would take Scott another sixty years, and having a highly successful business career, before he would top these academic achievements.

Chapter 5
Entrepreneur in the Making

Armed with a solid university education, Scott was primed and ready to hit the employment market upon graduation. "My dad wanted me to take my degree and get a job with a big company," Scott recalls. "He thought that if you weren't working, you weren't making money, and that if you weren't employed by someone, you didn't have job security. But I found ways of working both smarter and harder, and he finally warmed up to my ideas when I became successful." Though Scott would spend the first two decades after college gaining knowledge and experience in the world of conventional employment, he would constantly be on the lookout for opportunities that would lead him to his ultimate fate: becoming an entrepreneur.

In the Service

While Scott was still attending college, running his dive shop, and starting a family with his exotic French bride, he was also serving in the National Guard. "I could see the draft coming, the Bay of Pigs Invasion had just happened, I had friends who were joining, and so I signed up in 1963." He first went to Fort Knox, Kentucky, for eight weeks of boot camp followed by sixteen weeks of on-the-job training. He was based out of Ishpeming, but did his annual two-weeks' service at Camp Grayling in Grayling, a city located in Michigan's northern Lower Peninsula, about 260 miles (a four-hour drive) from Ishpeming.

In the summer of 1967, Scott, his wife, and their first child arrived at Camp Graying for his annual service, but no one was there. "They were all called up and sent to Detroit to help out with the street riots," Scott explains. Without a car, he could do little but board a military truck and leave Martine and their child at Camp Grayling while he headed off to Detroit—leaving it to Scott's parents to pick them up and bring them home.

The summer of 1967 hosted what has been called "the summer of rage" and "the '67 race riots." Riots broke out across over one hundred and fifty American cities spread across a huge swath of the nation: from Atlanta to Boston, Buffalo to Tampa, and New York City to Minneapolis, to name a few. The riots were a watershed moment in America's Civil Rights Movement (1954–1968), and no flashpoint was hotter or more destructive than the riots in the city of Detroit.

Scott and his fellow guardsmen were the tip of the spear.

While deployed in Detroit, Scott had mostly good experiences with the public, although while marching down Little Mack Avenue with bayonets affixed, they were shot at by snipers from the rooftops. "We had to be out there on the street for a certain number of hours; then we came back to a school on Little Mack where we rested for an hour," he reports. Their job was enforcing the curfew. Scott gratefully acknowledges, "The local residents were victims of the terrible destruction and violence. I remember that they brought us food, they laundered our clothes—they were glad we were there. I was in Detroit for a total of three weeks, and then we were moved on to Dearborn."

Scott was among seven thousand military called to the scene of what was one of the most deadly and destructive of the 1967 riots. The Detroit riots lasted five days and were marked by arson, looting, vandalism, and widespread violence: 43 dead, over 340 injured, and 1,400 buildings set ablaze. The National Guard sent to the scene was federalized and put under the authority of a regular US Army general. Scott was not impressed. "So there we were, with our rifles, out on the street, under occasional fire, and this 'genius' general tells the newspapers that we had no ammo in our guns and were not allowed to carry live rounds—just the kind of thing we wanted the armed looters and gangs to know!" Scott discharged from the Reserves in 1969.

Grown-Up Jobs

In 1966 Scott took his newly minted degrees and got a job with a big company, just like his father had suggested. He became a sales rep for the Upjohn Company, a prominent Michigan pharmaceutical manufacturer. He was required to travel extensively, and with a newborn at home, he had to make a choice between family and career. He quit in 1969 and took a job with his alma mater, Northern Michigan University, in their public services division as an assistant conference director from 1970 to 1971. It was a good job that had him home every evening for dinner. All the while, he kept his dive business going. In addition to dive tourism, his reputation for underwater skills led to well-paying, though tough, commercial dive jobs—for example, clearing and extending large water intake infrastructures while literally diving in silty mud.

In 1970 he interviewed with a company called Lakeshore Inc., a mining, marine, and automotive parts manufacturer, and was offered a sales engineer job. He would spend the next four years setting up a national sales force from coast to coast, and he founded a machine shop to build things for customers. There he learned what he already knew: there are good bosses and bad bosses, and you can learn a lot from both. "I had a bad boss at Lakeshore," Scott shares. "I was being pushed to move to Farmington, Michigan, but I had no interest in working there. When we traveled together, my boss would put himself in first class and put his subordinates in coach—something that did not endear him to his employees. He and I went to Schenectady, New York, to make a sale to General Electric. We sat down with the buyer I'd been developing who had a purchase agreement ready to go. When the buyer slid the agreement across the table to me, my boss reached over and pulled it to himself and began taking over the discussion. Later, back at the corporate office, he claimed the sale as his personal success." Scott was not cut out for such corporate shenanigans and began looking for the door.

On the other side of that door, in 1974, Scott met Jack Bean, owner of Bay City Foundry. They met at Jack's Southfield, Michigan, office where he explained what they do at their foundry in Bay City. Jack had liked a business plan that Scott had put together for a machine shop. An unusual but memorable conversation ensued. Jack announced, "I'm a millionaire, you know." Scott replied, "Yes, I want to be one too." Jack said, "I'm Jewish, you know." Scott replied, "I'm a Methodist." They liked each other, and a second meeting was held in Jack's home. "He offered me a job at more than what I was being paid at Lakeshore as vice president. So I resigned from Lakeshore," Scott says with a satisfied smile.

Jack Bean sold Bay City Foundry to Midland-Ross, a Fortune 300 conglomerate based in Cleveland, Ohio, in 1977 with a requirement that Jack stay on as CEO for a long period of time. Scott was present and involved in the sale, and in the process got to know the corporate heads at Midland-Ross. "I ended up attending all the meetings at Midland-Ross on behalf of Jack and started giving all the regular reports from Bay City Foundry to Midland-Ross."

What followed was ten difficult years at Bay City Foundry's subsidiary, struggling to show a profit while Midland-Ross buried them in corporate cross-charges—an old trick to make a preferred part of the business look like a hero, while dumping their costs into another, less-favored division. On top of that, there were other "financial mistreatments" of Bay City Foundry to contend with.

The NASA Shuttle Crawler-Transporter Tread Shoes Sale

It was 1984 and NASA was riding high with the Space Shuttle. The Shuttle program had been in operation for three years, having had its maiden orbital flight in April of 1981—a mere eight years after the last flight of the Saturn V. It was a marvel of technology. Like the Saturn V, it was assembled in the Vehicle Assembly Building (VAB) and delivered to the launch pad on the Space Shuttle crawler-transporter. Even with relatively limited use, a mere fourteen round trips between the VAB and launch pad (not including aborted missions), the crawler-transporter tread shoes were having problems: they were cracking and needed to be replaced. Each shoe was seven and a half feet long and weighed 2,200 pounds. There were fifty-six shoes per track belt, and eight track belts per crawler. This was a big order for a company the size of Bay City Foundry, but they could supply the order. If Scott was able to land that particular piece of high-profile NASA business, he would increase the profile and value of Bay City Foundry substantially.

By chance, one of Scott's salesmen was on a flight together with a salesman from a direct competitor located in Milwaukee. Scott's salesman reported to Scott that the Milwaukee salesman bragged that he'd just landed a big contract for the tread shoe castings for the crawler-transporter.

Scott asked his salesman if he knew whether the bidding for the casting job was closed or not—he didn't. Scott and his team immediately began calling any number they could get for NASA procurement until they located the NASA buyer in charge of the tread shoes. The buyer informed them that they were still accepting bids. There was no time to lose: Scott put his best engineer on a plane to Florida, who received a set of drawings from NASA. There was no time for him to fly back to deliver them. He cut the drawings into segments that were eight-and-a-half-by-eleven inches so he could fax them back up to Bay City Foundry's design and industrial engineers, who taped them together into complete drawings. Scott also managed to procure the price NASA paid for the original tread shoes. His team worked quickly, costing out the order and submitting their bid to NASA. They won the contract!

Business school textbooks talk about "the quick and the dead" in business, and this is what they mean. Although speed is essential, a total commitment and engagement with your business is key. Scott explains, "Good entrepreneurs aren't just risk-takers, but they're analysists, intelligent risk-takers. And you take nothing for granted, leave no stone unturned in the quest to find business and delight your customers."

Chapter 6
Entrepreneur Made
1st State Bank and Bay Cast Foundry

1st State Bank in Saginaw

"Whenever I've had to fill out a form that asked what my occupation was, I would always write 'entrepreneur,'" Scott confesses, convinced like many others that entrepreneur best sums him up professionally. And entrepreneurialism was the impetus behind the creation of 1st State Bank. "My only reason for getting into the banking business was to make money," Scott explains. "A friend, who was a contractor, had bad banking experiences. Turned down for loans. In my case, the lending officer would receive the presentation, but the board would reject it. Who would invest in a rust-belt foundry, after all?" So, when invited to join a group of six or so other Michigan businessmen from the Bay area who were having similar problems, and who intended to create a community bank while other community banks were being gobbled up by the big banks, Scott eagerly joined the team. The irony is that Scott had once rejected banking! He'd applied to work for Manufacturers National Bank of Detroit and even received an employment offer. But the location in Detroit wasn't going to work for him, and banking didn't feel right either, so he turned it down. 1st State Bank has multiple locations, serves the Bay City area, and is dedicated to supporting small businesses and being a true community bank. Scott exited 1st State Bank in 2019.

Bay Cast Foundry

In spite of the high-visibility success of landing the NASA contract, the years from 1985 through 1987 were bad years for the foundry industry. So bad, in fact, that Midland-Ross had made the decision to begin selling off its various companies—Bay City Foundry included. Corporate asked Scott to bring them a plan for closing down the Bay City Foundry operation. He developed a plan and presented it in one of Midland-Ross's conference rooms to some execs where it was promptly rejected. Scott was told, "In a week and a half, you are going to have everyone fired and the place shut down." Scott asked, "What are we going to do about the open orders to our auto company clients? The US Navy? Our other customers?" Scott refused to do it on the spot. Midland-Ross decided to sweeten the pot: "Do it and we'll give you a year's salary for severance." Scott didn't budge: "I won't do it. We'll be sued by our customers for non-delivery." He knew these corporate execs were insulated and would never have to deal with the consequences, but as a sales leader, he was the face of the company to these customers. And if he simply announced that Bay Cast Foundry was just dropping their orders, Scott knew that he was finished in the business. No one would ever trust him again.

Scott made them a proposition: He would finish and

deliver existing customer orders (the ones they wanted to cancel) and give Midland-Ross $140,000 from the proceeds on the sales. Then, he would buy the land, buildings, and equipment for a total of $500,000. "I bought everything except the receivables." With no idea how he would come up with the remaining $360,000, he rented another building in Bay City, moved the equipment over to the new location, hired seventeen people off the street, and finished the castings orders faster than he could have at the existing Bay City Foundry—even with their trained employees. Then Midland-Ross asked Scott if he'd also buy their substantial receivables. He bought them and, one by one, collected on them. "From my collections on the receivables, plus the sale of the outstanding castings, I bought the business in February 1987." He changed the name to Bay Cast Foundry. Over the subsequent years, Scott, together with his sons, built Bay Cast Inc. into one of the world's largest independent suppliers of heavy-sectioned, finished steel castings from 1,000 to 70,000 pounds.

Scott has a very clear understanding of what his family is and should be, and from where he acquired the value-programming to support his beliefs. "I stayed close to home as a kid and adopted my dad's deep conviction for family values and principles, and the value of hard work, which Martine and I have endeavored to instill in our sons Scott Jr., Max, and Jason, and our nine grandchildren."

Scott and Martine's three sons worked around the Bay Cast facility when they were young. They also mowed lawns and did other tasks while going to school, and they never complained. "They wanted to work," Scott explains. "I never pushed them to follow in my footsteps, but they wanted to." Scott eventually sold the business to his sons. "I did not give them Bay Cast Inc., mind you—I sold it to them." The transaction was negotiated in November of 2005 when Scott and his sons were at deer camp. "They did their homework, and made sure that the price they paid for it made sense. That made me proud. They've become common-sense smart and business smart."

Bay Cast makes components for SpaceX.

They agreed on the numbers and the price, and the deal was done at the end of January 2006. "And I insisted that once the deal was done, I'm out. After that it is in the boys' hands. And I got out of their way and they're doing a great job."

Today Scott and Martine split their time rotating every two weeks or so between their homes in the UP and Freeland, Michigan, with a five-week winter holiday in the Cayman Islands.

Chapter 7
Enlightened Volunteerism

Practically from the day good fortune began flowing into Scott Holman's world, good will began flowing out. This took the usual forms: marriage and parenting, serving his country and community, winning for his employees, and sharing with friends his love of the outdoors with adventures in the UP, the Caribbean, and even on distant continents. But this wasn't enough for Scott. He felt compelled to have a bigger impact. And there was one pivotal event that gave Scott just the right platform for doing more . . . lots more: being named *Inc. Magazine's* "Entrepreneur of the Year."

National Turnaround Entrepreneur of the Year

Scott bought Bay Cast in 1987, but within four years, his turnaround of the company was so successful that *Inc. Magazine*, Ernst & Young, and Institute of American Entrepreneurs awarded him their 1991 National Turnaround Entrepreneur of the Year Award. It was in recognition of the successful and rapid turnaround of a failing steel foundry into a modern, world-class producer of large machined steel castings: Bay Cast Inc. and Bay Cast Technologies.

Inc. Magazine's 1991 "Entrepreneur of the Year" edition proclaimed on the cover, "From thousands of nominees, *Inc.*'s national panel of judges picks the winners." Page forty-six featured a large sidebar with Scott's write-up and a photo of him with his dog:

1991 Turnaround Entrepreneur: *Scott L. Holman, Bay Cast Inc. and Bay Cast Technologies, Bay City, Mich.*

It sounds like a Frank Capra movie: against a backdrop of takeovers and leveraged buyouts, Scott L. Holman struggles to save a moribund foundry from the scrap heap. By dint of persistence, he builds two thriving enterprises with combined sales of $12 million.

The story begins in 1978, when Midland-Ross Corp., a giant conglomerate, paid $8 million for Bay City Foundry Co. As interest rates soared and a recession bore down, the foundry dove into the red. To be close to the operation, Scott Holman, who became general manager in 1981, took up residence above the offices. In 1982 the foundry lost about $2 million on sales of $8 million. By 1984 losses stood at roughly $500,000.

Holman made a bid to buy the company in 1985. Cobbling together funds from the Small Business Administration, the State of Michigan, and a bank, plus $100,000 of his own, he offered Midland-Ross $2.8 million—asking that it take back a $500,000 note. "They laughed at it; they were asking $3.2 million," he says. Finally, after a year and a half of shopping around for a buyer, Midland-Ross returned to Holman. On the verge of signing an agreement, though, Midland-Ross went through a leveraged buyout. New management, predictably, put the deal on hold. Then, in the late fall of 1986, a decision came down: either cough up an all-cash deal, or we close the place right away.

Undaunted, Holman offered one final option: he'd take the work in process, the raw materials, and enough equipment to finish the castings—normally a three-month job. At the end of three months, he'd pay Midland-Ross $148,000 out of his earnings. Midland-Ross consented. The next day, Holman rented a building, hired seventeen people through a temporary agency, and Bay Cast Inc. and Bay Cast Technologies were in business. Within three months he had not only paid up and made a $400,000 deal for the rest of the company's assets but also had $400,000 in accounts receivable for working capital.

The new company's sales hit $3 million in 1987, its first year, and are projected to reach more than $12 million in 1990. Profitable since the first month, Bay Cast's earnings exceeded the industry average—as does the company's productivity.

"We're giving the area an economic and psychological boost," says the forty-nine-year-old. "If what's happening here encourages somebody to take a risk and be successful, that would be wonderful."

Scott edged out some prominent national names when he received the award, including James F. McCann's contemporaneous rescue of 800-FLOWERS Inc.

The recognition was in large part due to the game-changing nature of one of the industry's most vexing problems: meeting delivery dates. After Scott's takeover of the company, Bay Cast started hitting a nearly 100 percent on-time delivery rate. "In our industry, you become a hero because no one does it," Scott explained in an *Inc. Magazine* interview. He was on the board of the Steel Founders' Society of America at the time and scanned their industry-member surveys looking for ways to win, and delivering on time was at the top of the list. "It was clear: those of us who will succeed make sure we meet our deadlines." Borrowing a scheduling technique used by NASA, Scott distinguished Bay Cast as "the company that delivers on time."

"When Ernst & Young and *Inc. Magazine* awarded me their National Turnaround Entrepreneur of the Year Award, that led to a lot of requests for speaking engagements," Scott explains. "I once gave a speech, 'Running a Business in an Entrepreneurial Environment,' to Russian business leaders in a Kremlin conference room in Moscow." This speaking opportunity arose through a business advocacy organization that was organizing a delegation of business experts to go to Russia and talk about free-enterprise economics. When Scott learned about the trip, he reached out to the organization, introduced himself, mentioned that he was the recipient of the Turnaround Entrepreneur of the Year Award, explained what he'd done at Bay Cast, and offered to be one of their guest speakers. It seems that talented people taking over defunct and mismanaged factories was just what the doctor ordered for the collapsing Soviet economy. He was brought on as a speaker.

The visit happened in December of 1991, precisely at the time of the transition from the Soviet Union (USSR) to the Commonwealth of Independent States (CIS). The Moscow event agenda included two state dinners hosting international and local attendees and officials. The first banquet, hosted by Boris Yeltsin, was in a huge dining hall in the Kremlin—a standing dinner where guests walked around to different tables where they were served various foods. The second banquet was to be hosted by Mikhail Gorbachev, but he never showed. After that banquet, Scott's delegation walked out into Red Square to join the celebration that was ongoing there. Lenin's body had already moved out of his tomb and Scott and his group watched as the Soviet flag was brought down and the CIS flag was hoisted.

Russian newspaper article about Kremlin conference
Photo of Scott Holman

Scott parlayed the 1991 award into success for Bay Cast, but also to take on an expanded role in the business community. The notoriety had local, regional, and national leadership and business advocacy organizations seeking him out for speaking engagements and board seats.

SUPPORTING YOUNG ENTREPRENEURS AND ACHIEVERS

Jaycees

The Jaycees is an organization for people between the ages of eighteen and forty, founded in 1920. They claim to have helped ". . . more than 12 million young adults in the United States and about 20 million worldwide become leaders in their communities." Today, they have four hundred clubs in the United States.

Scott was president of the Iron Mountain Jaycees during the 1970s. "It was a very important part of my leadership development," Scott explains. "It taught me how to run meetings and give interesting and well-prepared speeches." Iron Mountain, Michigan, is a city of 7,500 people, eighty miles from Marquette on the Wisconsin border. Scott attended state-wide meetings teaching leadership and other business skills to its membership, whom the Jaycees's website describes as ". . . young people who are looking to make a difference in their lives, in the lives of others, and in the communities they are a part of."

Given his own experiences with bad bosses, Scott gave his time to this organization in order to ensure the next generation had solid role models and guideposts for becoming great leaders. The organization's mission has managed to move with the times, as they lately have become particularly challenging for the organization. Justin Wutzke, the 2020 national president, identifies an on-going battle against media and government-driven misperceptions that leadership is something that is not attainable by everyone. He states in a 2020 interview, "We as a society don't do a good job in making people believe in themselves. We live in a world where we shame ourselves and others, and deal with several mental health issues. Having an opportunity to personally grow and develop is very important and this is what young-sters need to understand."

Given Scott's own battle with an educational system that shamed him for the symptoms of his undiagnosed dyslexia, and how his exceptional self-confidence and belief in himself allowed him to not just raise himself up but to far surpass his peers, he no doubt left a lasting impression on the young people he encountered throughout the organization.

1st State Bank's RUBY Award

The year after Scott founded 1st State Bank in 2005, he and the 1st State Bank team were looking for ways to recognize the "upward, bright, and young" from the bank's surrounding community. Through the auspices of 1st State Bank, the RUBY Award was created for that purpose. The award honors the region's outstanding under-forty professionals who "have made their mark in their professions and are having an impact throughout the Great Lakes Bay Region," according to 1st State Bank's website. The qualifications and requirements for nominees are that they must be age thirty-nine or younger and must either work or live in Bay, Saginaw, or Midland counties.

There is an annual gala dinner where that year's ten

recipients are presented with their awards. Now in its nineteenth year, the RUBY Award has become a Great Lakes Bay Region institution. While this award no doubt helps imprint the bank's brand and positioning within the business community as "the bank for business," it also effectively transplants that Yooper SISU neighbors-helping-neighbors spirit to broader communities downstate.

BUSINESS ORGANIZATIONS

Steel Founders' Society of America (SFSA)

This 122-year-old technical trade association exclusively for steel foundries advocates for its members, represents their interests to regulators and external stakeholders, and provides members a convenient source of industry information. Specifically, SFSA has been summarized in its literature in this way: "Members benefit from SFSA's experience in steel technology development programs, market development, representing the industry globally in regulatory and specification development, and providing timely business information and state-of-the-art training."

Like all industries, steel casting is dealing with generational changes in the workforce, the continuous advent of new technologies, and always regulation, both domestic and international. To help its members stay on top of these things, the SFSA provides members access to a digital directory of members, a repository of reports and training resources, monthly training webinars, and the *Casteel Reporter* (a monthly digital publication covering sales, technology, etc.), and oversees an industry research budget of $3 million, among other activities.

Since Bay Cast resides precisely in the industry sweet spot, and given Scott's propensity for being named to leadership roles seemingly whenever they become available, Scott served as both director and board chairman during his relatively brief eight-year membership. All the more remarkable is that, engineers and technical experts being as they are, a science and technology industry association would name a leader whose degrees are in biology and business, and whose knowledge of the industry is effectively self-taught.

Chambers of Commerce

Scott Holman with Senator Fred Thompson

"Being part of a chamber of commerce is a great opportunity to learn from others," Scott shares with enthusiasm. "Think about it: you get to sit next to executives who manage huge companies and learn from them through their experiences." Scott has embraced this opportunity to develop a remarkably extensive personal and professional network locally, nationally, and internationally. To date, Scott has had thirty-two years of continuous involvement with the chamber of commerce at multiple levels and across multiple roles.

His initial engagement was at the Michigan Bay Area level, which began with becoming a member in 1992. Over the subsequent twelve years, Scott served stints as a director and vice-chairman of the Chamber. One of those huge companies Scott refers to is locally headquartered Dow Chemical. Naturally, the Bay Area Chamber of Commerce is committed to serving its Bay-area members and community by promoting a healthy and growing business environment leading to overall prosperity and a thriving community. Their stated focus: "People. Partnerships. Progress."

Two years later, in 1994, Scott became a member of the US Chamber of Commerce national organization and is still a member today. Likewise, for part of that time, he served as a director and vice-chairman. In addition, he had terms as chair for both the Regulatory Policy and Accreditation Committees. Considering the US Chamber of Commerce is the largest business organization and network in the world, this is the top of the chamber game. They describe the scale of their mission as ". . . the only organization that optimizes the relationship between government and business at scale, across the economy, and around the world."

In 2002 Scott became a Michigan Chamber of Commerce member and he served terms as both a director and chairman. The Michigan Chamber publicly positions itself as being "the most influential voice for business in Michigan." With over five thousand members that employ over a million people, this is a credible boast. Based in Lansing, the seat of Michigan state government, the organization certainly does have a voice with state regulators. Indeed, the Michigan Chamber of Commerce is so ardent in their pro-business advocacy that their website confidentially labels their Lansing Walnut Street address, "World Headquarters for Free Enterprise."

The most recent addition to Scott's chamber journey is joining the US Chamber Foundation in 2016, and again serving in a leadership role as director. The Chamber Foundation is a somewhat-different animal than the Chamber of Commerce itself. Its mission focuses on steering the resources and ingenuity of free enterprise toward altruistic problem-solving. Most prominent of these is their work in the area of disaster relief. An example of how this operates is where business supply-chain experts help non-profit relief organizations more effectively deploy supplies to disaster areas. Other areas include a focus on teaching "civil literacy" to the next generation of Americans, helping close the gap between education and career readiness, skills-based hiring practices to improve overall organizational development, and leadership development. The mission of the US Chamber Foundation aligns well with Scott's current interests, which are focused on more altruistic and philanthropic endeavors.

NON-BUSINESS ORGANIZATIONS

Great Lakes Shipwreck Historical Society

Who better than Scott Holman to serve twelve years on the board of the Great Lakes Shipwreck Historical Society? After all, Scott was the Lake Superior recreational scuba pioneer who ran wreck diving expeditions out of nearby-Marquette. He fit right in with the group of divers, teachers, and educators who founded the organization in 1978 for the purpose of exploring historic shipwrecks in eastern Lake Superior.

A non-profit organization, its stated mission is to "preserve lights and stations which warned mariners of the dangers inherent; honor those who were aboard and who bravely attempted rescue; and discover, document, and interpret vessels which instead took the deep." It oversees some of the most historic and important sites on its end of the Upper Peninsula, including the historic Whitefish Point and Light Station, the Great Lakes Shipwreck Museum, the Soo Locks Park, and a US Weather Bureau building.

The Whitefish Point Light Station, constructed in 1861, is the oldest operating lighthouse on the lake. It was added to the National Register of Historical Places in 1973. The Great Lakes Shipwreck Museum displays the bell of the ship *Edmund Fitzgerald*, which was recovered from the wreck in 1995 via a joint expedition that included the Great Lakes Shipwreck Historical Society, the National Geographic Society, the Royal Canadian Navy, Sony Corporation, and the Sault Ste. Marie tribe of Chippewa Indians. The historical society owns and operates *RV David Boyd*, a three-person underwater research vessel with the mission to document and access the lake's wrecks. Filled with state-of-the-art gear and equipment, it is often used to assist law enforcement and environmental agencies.

As we will see in the next chapter, preservation of Upper Peninsula historical sites is a particular passion of Scott's, one to which he continues to dedicate the latter years of his life.

Mackinac Center for Public Policy (MCPP)

The core mission for the MCPP is "advancing liberty and opportunity for all people . . . [to] free people to realize their potential and their dreams." The organization describes itself as a non-profit public policy research and educational institution. They are focused on promoting free markets and limited government and do so through advocacy for public policy. Scott was a member since its founding in 1987 and has remained a member supporter and on the board of advisors for nearly thirty years.

Besides the critical (but less tangible) role of providing a pragmatic perspective to the quilt of the Michigan public policy zeitgeist, there were demonstrable results from the organization's advocacy.

With the advent of GPS and modern digital navigation tools, coastal lighthouses have become increasingly less important critical infrastructure for ensuring maritime safety. Ships, for example, no longer needed to risk sailing within sight of shores and lighthouses. This, of course, obviated the need for incurring the expense of maintaining strings of lighthouses along coastlines. As they were sequentially closed, they would inevitably fall into disrepair and eventually disappear altogether, losing an important part of Michigan's history. The National Historic Lighthouse Preservation Act of 2000, legislation sponsored by Michigan's US Senator Carl Levin, is one example of how local advocacy can have national impact. While Scott and Martine's acquisition of the Granite Island Lighthouse Station preceded the legislation's passage by a year, the organization's advocacy was certainly influential in motivating the federal government to preserve Michigan's precious and always-beautiful Great Lakes historical lighthouses.

MCPP's passionate advocacy for the constitutionally rooted viewpoint that "governments don't create prosperity, people do," and that governments have a proper role in the course of human events to ensure the blessings of liberty, aligns not only with Scott's belief, but his entire life experience. His third-of-a-century commitment to the organization demonstrates that.

Torch Club

The International Association of Torch Clubs is an international (US-Canadian) association created to facilitate open discussions of wide-ranging topics, from current events to history and folklore. Now entering their one-hundredth year, the organization seeks members from eclectic backgrounds, professions, and viewpoints in order to maximize benefit to their members. They meet for dinners and happy-hours and hold in-person meetings and conventions. They also publish *The Torch* magazine seasonally, which states, "Torch is about dialogue . . . where you are invited to share your knowledge, your experience, and your perspective with other professionals in an ideal social setting." The magazine serves as an additional tool for facilitating that dialogue between members. Given Scott's leadership experience, executive presence, and experience leading various associations, the Torch Club International-Saginaw chapter saw fit to make him their director and president during part of Scott's thirty-seven-year membership there. He remains a member today.

NORTHERN MICHIGAN UNIVERSITY

Though Scott graduated from Northern Michigan University in 1965 with two degrees, graduation was only the beginning of his life-long relationship with the university. It started, of course, as an employee of the university with his stint from 1970 to 1971 as assistant conference director at NMU's public services division. Later he held several executive roles, including president of the NMU Alumni Association and as a member of the College of Business Board. Accolades include receiving the Distinguished Alumni Award and having his name affixed to two rooms on campus: the Scott L. Holman Executive Conference Room and the Scott L. Holman Case Study Room. Among these and various financial donations, the two areas where Scott made significant and lasting contributions to the standing and long-term viability of the university were his tenure on the board of trustees (which included two stints as chairman), and his philanthropic work (e.g., making his Granite Island Lighthouse available to the university).

NMU Board of Trustees

Northern Michigan University's Board of Trustees is a governing board consisting of eight members appointed by Michigan's governor. The university describes the board's function as "[providing] general supervision of the institution, the control and direction of all expenditures from the institution's funds, and such other powers and duties as prescribed by law." Today Scott is a trustee emeritus as of January 2019, and the university's stated requirements for emeritus status eligibility begins to describe his many contributions over the years. From the NMU website:

> To be eligible [for emeritus status], the former member shall have achieved certain contributions to the university similar to but not limited to the following types of activities:
>
> - Participation in and contributions to Board of Trustee meetings and committees, and working on Board of Trustee efforts away from meetings;
> - Time and effort on behalf of the university in areas like student recruitment, student retention, lobbying elected officials, hosting off-campus NMU events, and, when called upon, acting as an ambassador for the university;
> - Time and effort in attending university functions both on and off campus;

- Time and effort on behalf of the NMU Alumni Association and its committees;
- Assistance to the NMU Foundation, e.g., making referrals of likely donors, personal financial support, securing estate/trust gifts, etc.;
- Time, effort, and financial support of Friends of NMU.

Over the decades, Scott has ticked most of these boxes.

Scott was initially appointed to the board for a term that lasted from 1997 to 2005, and was elected chairman of the NMU Board of Trustees in 1999. Years later, by appointment of Governor Snyder, Scott returned to the board in 2014 after a protracted absence. The appointment would take him through the year 2018 and would incorporate another chairman assignment in 2017. With Scott's return, NMU's President David Haynes said, "We welcome back former Board Chair Scott Holman. Mr. Holman is also a proud Northern alumnus who has stayed actively engaged with Northern Michigan University in a wide variety of ways, so I know he is going to continue to be a strong advocate for moving NMU forward as a member of the board."

Putting NMU on the Scientific Map

The Granite Island Light Station that Scott purchased in 1999 is about twelve miles out into Lake Superior from the NMU campus, and this NMU newsletter excerpt best explains his actions and motives for making NMU a beneficiary and stakeholder in the rehabilitation and repurposing of the island:

September 23, 2013: NMU Gains Ownership of Weather Station

> "About five years ago, a University of Nebraska professor was looking for a unique place to put the equipment and approached me about using the island," said Holman. "I said, 'If I let you do this, you have to involve an NMU student in the research.' Then earlier this year, I suggested NMU should take the lead on this and actually assume

ownership of the equipment. The WiMAX [Worldwide Interoperability for Microwave Access] and weather station fit together because you need internet to transmit data back to the mainland. They played a pivotal role in NMU's groundbreaking WiMAX network, which is now the Educational Access Network."

The weather research station put NMU on the map for atmospheric and environmental research. Their Granite Island Weather Station became part of a five-station Great Lakes Integrated Sciences and Assessments Center. The newsletter describes NMU's role: "Professors and students are able to monitor and assess air temperature, relative humidity, barometric pressure, evaporation, carbon dioxide, wind speed and direction, precipitation, solar radiation, and water temperature." This amounts to an invaluable and rare collegiate opportunity to get hands-on with the science and methodology students will encounter when they enter the real world, whether in academia, government, or business.

June 15, 2018: NMU-NASA Granite Island Project Underway

Scott's donations and advocacy even brought NASA to NMU! With NASA's equipment installed, the Granite Island station measures offshore solar radiation for NASA's "Clouds and the Earth's Radiant Energy System" (CERES) experiments. In a nutshell, the ground station validates NASA's satellite readings—critical for calibration and accuracy.

Again, from the NMU newsletter:

"Granite Island was selected as a CERES site based on its over-water location, as well as the available infrastructure, power, and internet at the island," said John Lenters, NMU research associate and owner of Lentic Environmental Services. "The potential added benefit of weather monitoring equipment that had been installed at the island previously as part of the Great Lakes Evaporation Network also appealed to NASA."

Whether it was his many years of service on the NMU Board of Trustees or personally ferrying students out to Granite Island in unpredictable waters, NMU assesses Scott's contributions to the university in this way: "His philanthropy has made a lasting impact on his alma mater as well by facilitating scholarships, research initiatives, and campus infrastructure enhancement."

Scott sums up how the university fits into his life: "Twenty-six family members have graduated from NMU, going back to 1926. Between that and my service on the alumni board and as a trustee, I feel a sense of proprietorship in a way. That's what makes me want to stay involved with Northern and help when I see an opportunity."

Chapter 8
Preserving Michigan's UP Treasures

Granite Island Light Station

Restored Granite Island Lighthouse

Lake Superior, the deepest and northernmost lake of North America's five Great Lakes, contains 10 percent of the earth's surface's fresh water. It straddles the forty-eighth parallel between the United States and Canada and is a notoriously dangerous body of water. Atmospheric conditions at that latitude, combined with the massive size and depth of the lake, make for sudden, powerful squalls and unpredictable large, choppy waves. Native Americans who followed the retreating ice sheet north ten thousand years ago knew all too well the ferocious and unforgiving nature of Lake *Gitche Gumee* when braving its waves in their dugout canoes.

When the fur trade brought the first Europeans to the region in numbers during the 1700s, they took their cues from the locals, learning to be cautious and respectful of the lake. Indeed, the saying that Lake Superior never gives up its dead has its basis in the lake's barely-above-freezing temperature: the cold water suppresses bacterial growth in bodies, preventing the gas bloating that normally brings dead bodies up to the surface. It must have been intimidating knowing that, when angered, the lake swallows its victims whole, never to be seen again.

Larger ships of nineteenth-century industry began plying the lake's waters in support of the timber industry. By the time of the American Civil War, the Lake Superior region was the nation's leading timber producer. Shortly thereafter, even more massive steamships began to arrive in service to the copper industry along the Keweenaw Peninsula and mining of iron ore in Michigan's Upper Peninsula and as far away as Minnesota's Mesabi Range. Unlike sailing ships, steamships didn't need to wait for favorable winds or mild conditions, so their operating range on the lake was much broader. But this also increased the risk of being caught by Superior's ill temperament when steaming between mining ports and the Soo Locks (opened in 1855) that linked Superior to the other four Great Lakes—routes that took these ships right past the city of Marquette.

Both transiting ships and those that docked at Marquette itself threaded a needle between the rocky coast and the ofttimes-raging waves out on the lake. As early as the 1830s, *Na-Be-Quon* Island, a two-and-a-half-acre, sixty-foot-high rocky outcropping twelve miles northeast of Marquette City, was recognized as a landmark obstacle. But by 1867 it was recognized as an opportunity to improve navigational safety. Consequently, $20,000 was approved by the US Congress for the construction of a lighthouse. Granite Island, as it is called in English, had a forty-foot-high steel tower and a 2,400-square-foot keeper's quarters built on its peak. The lighthouse sports a white fourth-order Fresnel lens and, owing to frequent thick fog in the area, a second-hand fog bell from Thunder Bay Island.

During the lighthouse's early years, it likely used one or more of the illuminants of the day: whale oil, lard, or kerosine. In 1905 an oil house was built to support oil vapor as an illuminant, and in 1937 the lighthouse was further upgraded to use the much-brighter acetylene. In 1939 the US Coast Guard took over the lighthouse service, removed the keeper's quarters furnishings, and operations were automated. The light station was eventually shut down sometime in the mid-1940s.

Then, in 1999, the US Coast Guard deemed the Granite Island Lighthouse to be redundant and put both the lighthouse and the island itself up for auction. Scott won ownership of the island with an $86,003 bid. Scott and Martine were now the proud owners of a rock island with a weathered and worn-out building on top that they fully intended to restore to its glory days—even better. The lighthouse quarters were listed on the National Register of Historic Places in 1983 and demanded to be rescued.

Uniquely, Scott knew Granite Island like the back of his hand. He personally visited the island in his youth and knew the area both above and below the water, having dove to numerous shipwrecks in the surrounding waters. He'd last set foot on the island in 1963. Still, Granite Island has its perils.

Granite Island after winter thaw

The weather could significantly change for the worse during the twelve-mile boat journey to the island. Isaac Bridges, the first Granite Island Lighthouse keeper who was there the day it was first lit, drowned in a boating accident in 1872. Twenty-six years later, keeper William Wheatley also drowned while on the lake during one of its notorious sudden storms. And, in 1903, wind drove keeper's assistant John McMartin's boat onto the rocks, where he also drowned. But Scott would not be deterred by fear, superstition, or the monumental restoration task ahead.

Restoration

Naturally, the stone structure was in good condition, but the top floor's wooden roof had collapsed and the elements had their way with the inside of the keeper's quarters. Some of the original first-floor wood framework was still in good condition, and what could be salvaged was. In 2000 an existing water-side 1903-model derrick crane was reconditioned and put back in service, unloading equipment and restoration materials from boats at the newly installed suspended steel dock. Stairs were built from the shoreline up the rocky slope for the construction crew and visitors.

Transporting the requisite tools, materials, and people to Granite Island's remote and sometimes-hazardous location during a short season was the single most vexing challenge of the entire restoration. The project required no less than two standard Zodiac boats, a thirty-foot Zodiac 920 with a cabin, and a 1946 gillnet commercial fishing boat, the *Oluf Mechelson*. The logistics problem was solved, but another challenge loomed: engaging skilled people to do the restoration work.

Finding a Marquette contractor who would do the job was another major challenge. None of the ones he managed to get out there for inspection were interested in bidding on the job. Scott would need to improvise. If he couldn't find a construction crew to work on the project, he'd have to mobilize one. Scott hired Stan Stenson, a carpenter from the town of Covington, sixty miles (one-hour's drive) west of Marquette, to assemble a team of craftsmen for the project. Living in tents while making the initial major repairs to the roof and second floor, the team gutted the building of its 130-year-old plaster walls and replaced them with modern sheetrock. Stan's carpentry skills came in handy when hand-making historically correct doors and windows. The station was electrified with modern state-of-the-art electrical equipment and connected to wind and solar power generators, giving the island an independent and renewable power source—with more-than-adequate battery capacity. A five-thousand-watt propane generator was installed for back-up. Power management on the island is remotely controlled year-round. Its weather station data is accessible though the WiMAX system for global connectivity. Live, real-time, internet web cameras are operated by Northern Michigan University and accessible to all.

Scott at the Granite Island Weather Station

Thinking back on this challenging and difficult restoration project, Scott reports, "I made hundreds of trips ferrying contractors to and from the island, and the total repair bill was in the six figures. I'm telling you this, you cannot restore a lighthouse with bake sales. I just can never get over the fact that they built this whole darned thing in one summer, and it took me two and a half summers to repair it with all the materials and technology we have today."

Mt. Shasta

The Granite Island Lighthouse isn't the only UP treasure that Scott rescued from time and neglect. The Mt. Shasta Restaurant, located in Michigamme, Michigan, is another. Like Granite Island, Scott had ties to the place. Among his public statements on Mt. Shasta, he said, "It's got a lot of history, a lot of memories; a lot of people have made friendships here, and it goes back to a little family history that I have." From a 2018 interview by local television station WLUC's Julie Williams, "The 1959 movie adaptation of *Anatomy of a Murder* was shot around Marquette County, including Mt. Shasta, meaning the likes of Duke Ellington and Jimmy Stewart have walked the restaurant's floors." Scott says, "I remember going behind Mt. Shasta and greeting the actors as they came back from the shoot. I got a book signed by all the actors." And Scott wasn't the only Holman who had attachments to the Mt. Shasta Restaurant: "My dad grew up in Michigamme. . . . Morris [the owner at the time] and my mother and dad were friends during their lifetime, and they just ran a wonderful restaurant. People have a lot of great memories. It used to be a place where people would come in and it was almost like a Friday night reunion for friends in the area." After having been closed for three years between owners, Scott saw his chance to recreate and preserve that special part of UP culture. He was determined to bring it back. Scott acquired Mt. Shasta Restaurant in July 2018.

Michigamme

The Mt. Shasta building was originally built in Scott's hometown of Ishpeming in 1935, then was broken down and moved twenty-three miles to the north shore of Lake Michigamme. The log cabin portion of the building was built in 1935 in Ishpeming as part of a WPA[1] project. It sat idle and the builder needed to sell it. In 1939 a new owner broke it down, trucked it to Michigamme, reassembled it, and opened it for business, moving between bar-restaurant and restaurant-bar formats over the years.

It [Michigamme] is a bright, active mining town of 1,800 inhabitants, and derives its resources from several of the leading mines on the range. The site of the town borders on the west end of Lake Michigamme (Great Lake), and the surrounding scenery is very beautiful. The waters of the lake encircle many pretty and picturesque islands, and the scene, as a whole, is one that vividly impresses the mind with its wonderful natural beauty.

— Source unknown, circa 1883

* * *

MICHIGAMME IS FROM THE OJIBWE LANGUAGE, AND, like a lot of Upper Peninsula towns, got its start in timber, sawmills, and mining. The discovery of almandine (an iron alumina garnet) in 1872 birthed what was originally called the Mt. Shasta Mine—later renamed the Michigamme Mine. By 1873 the little town of Michigamme swelled to three hundred people. And like many mining towns, it went through a series of boom-and-bust cycles, relying on high seasonal incomes to supplement long idle periods. In modern times, Michigamme, and UP communities like it, rely heavily on tourism: summer and winter outdoor activities, from mountain biking to snowmobiling.

Importantly, Michigamme is located thirty-eight miles (a forty-five-minute drive) west of Marquette, close enough for Marquette's 68,000 residents (and visitors during the summer months) to drive over to this UP landmark for lunch or dinner. Like the Granite Island Lighthouse, recognizing the wasted potential that an idle Mt. Shasta represented for Michigamme's 255 year-round residents, Scott and Martine were determined to bring it back to its glory days—even better.

Renovation

The building got a new roof and floor, new wiring and plumbing, and new appliances under a new, redesigned layout. It has a large stone fireplace and outdoor picnic-style dining. Its charm is its rustic log cabin restaurant and lounge areas. It opens for the summer starting in May and closes its doors completely every winter. Unlike Granite Island, the renovation took only three months. After hiring and training staff, Mt. Shasta reopened its doors September 2018 as a casual-fine dining restaurant. "I think if you were to look around and see the atmosphere, you would enjoy it," Scott says.

In tribute to its illustrious history as a location scene for the Oscar-nominated *Anatomy of a Murder*, over fifty photographs of the stars, including Jimmy Stewart, Lee Remick, and Eve Arden, among others, adorn the walls. The piano played by Duke Ellington in the movie is there for patrons' enjoyment. But all the glitz and glamor are an aside for Scott. He explains why he made the effort to preserve the restaurant for new generations: "Reopening the restaurant is an important source of income for the people of Michigamme and will help improve people's lives there." Spoken in true neighborly Yooper spirit.

Chapter 9
PERMA

*Positive psychology takes you through the
countryside of pleasure and gratification,
up into the high country of strength and
virtue, and finally to the peaks of lasting
fulfillment, meaning, and purpose.*

— Dr. Martin Seligman, creator of the
PERMA Model, 2002

I n 2011 Dr. Seligman hypothesized that PERMA
(Positive Emotion, Engagement, Relationships, Meaning, and Accomplishment) represents the elements of
well-being, the five characteristics of a flourishing individual.[1]
With this tool we plot anecdotal as well as demonstrable
evidence acquired through the testimony of those who know
Scott best, and Scott himself, to map the source of his

entrepreneurial spirit that has fueled his success and personal fulfillment.

Positive Emotions

Scott and Martine are consummate entertainers. According to a friend and colleague, one place to see Scott's ability to project positivity is at one of his shindigs. "Once, at a Fourth of July party he was hosting, I couldn't help but marvel at the extraordinary effort he went to to ensure the guests were well-taken care of, happy, and enjoying themselves, from the catering to the service. It was amazing. Meticulous planning and execution. Also amazing was the eclectic mix of the guests who attended. That didn't just happen; he did that deliberately, structured it that way. And the same was true at another gathering he organized at the King Lake home. Outstanding."

"Scott is optimistic about the future, and he projects that," explains a Michigan Chamber of Commerce Board colleague. "When we served together on the chamber board, one of the things I noticed was that Scott and Martine were very warm and friendly to me and my wife. When we met, it was warm, friendly, with a lot of hugging. They were wonderful people to be around."

Engagement

"When I think about engagement, I think about how I was blessed to be associated with the Michigan Chamber since the mid-1980s," Scott's Michigan Chamber of Commerce colleague shares. "I traveled to all eighty-three Michigan counties, big cities and small, and met many Michiganders in the process. When you are asked to be the chairman, it isn't by chance, and everyone knew Scott had what it took to fill the role of chairman. What I found remarkable about his leadership was his passion. He could be emotional at times, but in a positive way: 'How can we change things? How can we make this better?' Scott understood from his humble beginnings that if you want to avoid mistakes, do nothing. But he knew Michigan couldn't succeed by standing still. Scott was fearless! He had his own systematic decision-making process. As long as he was on the mission to make Michigan business better, he was all-in. Inaction and lack of vision is bad; action is good."

"Scott was successful in a fiercely competitive business, Bay Cast," a chamber colleague says. "Business was down in the early 1980s and Scott was looking for opportunities to land orders that would utilize capacity and improve the top line. Nothing better demonstrates Scott's level of engagement than his company landing a particular piece of high-profile NASA business."

Relationships

One of Scott's King Lake neighbors, Dr. Greg Messenger, a dermatologist in Lansing who owns an adjacent property, explains the essence of relationships in that part of rural America. "There is a certain decorum [unwritten rule] when your closest neighbor is three miles away for when your neighbor needs something, needs your help: If you're stuck outside in the winter, you can go into someone's cabin or home to get food and start a fire to get warm. Under such conditions, your neighbor is automatically your friend." And it wasn't a rule that only applied to crisis situations; it was a part of everyday life. "I own a lake near Scott's and have to go through his property to get to my property, and vice versa. We just come across each other while crossing each other's properties. We were bonded together by our common love: the UP. When Scott would come up north by himself, we'd have him come over for dinner." It is this kind of rapport that is the cultural foundation upon which Scott builds his relationships that extend not only beyond the UP, Michigan, and the United States, but in other places around the world.

One chamber of commerce colleague says, "Sometimes extraordinarily successful people don't want two-way relationships. Often it is only one way: from themselves. But

Scott is a deliberate listener and learner from other people, and builds relationships with them to facilitate that. Consequently, people would seek him out for advice and counsel precisely because he has two-way conversations."

"Scott has a very good moral compass," reports Rich Studley, Scott's fellow Michigan Chamber of Commerce board member. "He put his arm around me, coached me, guided me when I took over as CEO of a state-wide organization with these words: 'Be the keeper of the mission. Be faithful to our vision, mission, and values. Do the right thing for our members.'"

"Relationships and business success go hand-in-hand," one friend observes. "Scott artfully blends the professional and the personal, to great effect—both in his business success and the sincerity of his personal relationships."

* * *

When asked by a reporter what he would do if he were suddenly broke, John D. Rockefeller responded, "I would borrow a nickel to make a phone call."

— Attribution lost to history

* * *

"RELATIONSHIPS ARE KEY," SCOTT SHARES. "YOU NEED them to help solve the problems that you can't do on your own." And Scott has endeavored to pass this learning on to the next generation. "I've tried to impress upon my children how important it is to make relationships with people on those chambers of commerce and various boards that I sat on. They were essential to making productive business connections."

Meaning

As described in this book's foreword, the "Meaning" dimension includes people dedicating themselves to something greater than themselves. It is doing things that are meaningful to them. Scott's entire trip to Russia as a guest speaker at a Kremlin conference was certainly that—including a side trip to Berlin. Scott says, "I was proud to do my part to help the Russian people, our former enemy who suffered under communism, to learn how to create value though entrepreneurship. There was a lot of business travel over the years, but I never lost the opportunity to add a little personal time on the side. On that trip, when in Berlin, I took a piece of the Berlin Wall myself, with a hammer and chisel. For a veteran of the Cold War era, that really meant something."

Rich Studley says, "As a board member of the Michigan Chamber of Commerce, Scott was always supportive of members' interests. He would always say, 'What is the right things to do?' Not the most expedient or safest thing to do. If there is one thing I learned from Scott, it is to always do your homework, and be prudent yet not afraid to take calculated risks. If you want to make a big difference in the world, you have to take prudent risks."

One thing that means the world to Scott is the prospect of

helping ease the burden of his fellow dyslexics by improving the educational system itself. He is currently formulating a plan to recruit experts from the dyslexic medical and educational world, specifically Yale University researchers among others, to create a research and learning center for dyslexia at Northern Michigan University. "And the learning will include teaching teachers in addition to students," Scott eagerly shares. "The focus will be on discovering what you can do, not just what you can't do. And from there, students and teachers can develop the workarounds to help these students effectively live and succeed in spite of their dyslexia." This would include a book that Scott would like to write under the auspices of the university, naturally entitled *Overcoming Dyslexia*.

Accomplishments

By far Scott's greatest personal accomplishment, the one that is most precious to him, is receiving his honorary doctoral degree in business from Northern Michigan University in December 2023. This kid who was "too dumb for second grade" had not only earned bachelor's degrees in both biology and business, but he now held a doctorate degree. The most meaningful comment that Scott received on the special day he received his doctorate was from his wife Martine: "Your teachers said you were a daydreamer and look at you now: you daydreamed and then chose to live your dream."

* * *

WINNERS HAVE WINNING MINDSETS AND THERE IS NO doubt that Scott possesses one, though he cautions that, along with winning, there are risks: "The profit you make is commensurate with the risks that you take. Great leadership leads to more intelligent risk-taking. When you have to lead a group in a certain direction, you will need to take chances that others may not think are wise. But you have to take risks, including financial risks, because that's the only way you're going to get a payoff."

Scott offers this thought on finding solutions: "If you're working on a solution, and there are two paths that you could take, choose your 'A' preferred option, but always have a good 'Plan B.' That way you win whether you end up taking 'A' or 'B'."

Chapter 10
The Right Stuff
Jerry Linenger: NASA Astronaut and Mir Cosmonaut

Captain Jerry Linenger is a retired United States Navy flight surgeon, medical research principal investigator, and NASA astronaut. A US Naval Academy graduate, Dr. Jerry Linenger also holds two doctorates (medicine and epidemiology), two master's degrees (systems management and policy), as well as three honorary doctorates of science. Astronaut Linenger flew Space Shuttle missions aboard Discovery and Atlantis. During what has been reported to be one of the most dangerous and dramatic missions in space history, he spent nearly five months aboard the Russian space station Mir, where the crew survived the worst fire ever aboard an orbiting spacecraft.[1] His media work includes: NBC News correspondent for the "Today Show" and "Nightly News"; numerous guest appearances on FOX, CBS, CNN, and PBS; consultant to, and featured on-air in, various History Channel, IMAX, Discovery, and HBO films and documentaries, as well as the acclaimed Nat Geo documentary, *One Strange Rock*, now on Netflix/Disney+; and local, national, and international radio appearances. Jerry's authored two books: *Off the Planet*, about being in space, and *Letters from Mir: An Astronaut's Letters to His Son*.[2] For his service to his country in the space program, NASA awarded him the Distinguished Service Medal. Jerry fondly shares his experience with Scott Holman here.

I'M A PROUD MICHIGANDER. I WAS BORN AND RAISED IN Detroit, graduated from East Detroit High School, and received my doctorate in medicine from Wayne State University School of Medicine. My career in the Navy took me all over the world and I lived abroad for extended periods in places such as the Philippines. NASA also had me moving around quite a bit between various NASA training centers in the United States, outside the country, like at the Gagarin Cosmonaut Training Center in Star City, Russia, and, of course, 143 days in space. But the draw from Michigan was too great and I eventually returned to Michigan. And that's where I had the privilege of meeting Scott Holman, developing a wonderful friendship and sharing our love of Northern Michigan and adventure together.

We met up in the UP after I came back from a space flight. NASA had me doing post-flight talks, as it has astronauts do, and since I'm from Michigan, I was sent there to do that. I thought to do some speaking in the UP, at Northern

Michigan University in Maquette, and that's where I met Scott. He is not only an NMU alumni, but also a board member and past chairman. We hit it off right away and have become good friends.

Over the years, our friendship has blossomed in many ways, and I've had the privilege of getting to know Scott's amazing wife, Martine, and their wonderful sons, too. When I coached Traverse City's hockey team, and an away game took us near Bay City, I'd take the players to visit Bay Cast so they could learn how things are made. Scott took me diving in the Cayman Islands. And, of course, we spend time at his King Ranch. Often, after we've had extensive and far-reaching conversations, I reflect on his insights, thoughts, and comments when driving back home. Scott always gives me a lot to think about. I always learn from Scott, to look at things from different angles. I've observed him in debates where he's on the polar-opposite side of something, but he never gets overbearing and always attacks the logic of a person's argument, never the person.

Having been involved in naval aviation and the astronaut corps, you can imagine that I've been around some high-quality people over my career. This includes high-ranking naval officers entrusted to lead carrier strike groups of 7,500 people consisting of the carrier, destroyers, cruisers, and even submarines, to fellow astronauts, many of whom are top in their field—from Nobel Prize-winning astrophysicists to top Navy pilots, and, of course, the proverbial rocket scientists themselves. I can tell you that Scott can hold his own in these groups—he is an equally high-quality and highly competent person.

When I got into the astronaut corps, I was surrounded by those over-the-top smart people because it was NASA: a magnet for the world's best talent, its most exceptional people. There you expect to see that top-flight excellence all around you. But there is Scott, a regular guy running a foundry in Bay City, Michigan, a restauranteur and hunting retreat owner in Northern Michigan, and he is 100 percent in the same league as those NASA guys. I grew up blue collar, so I have a special appreciation for what Scott has been able to achieve in his life. After years of having the opportunity to spend time with Scott, I've considered what puts Scott in that class and have summarized the attributes into seven areas of skill, expertise, and competence:

1. *An Engineer's Mind.* I hold a master's degree in systems management and a doctorate in research methodology. Based on that academic training, combined with everything I've learned about systems methodology and processes as a naval aviator and in the astronaut corps, what Scott has achieved just at Bay Cast alone is remarkable. He took a dying operation and completely turned it around. Filling NASA contracts puts you in league with the big boys of Space Inc., and Bay Cast is a go-to company in that respect. He's made highly complex machinery and processes work on the shop floor, so much so that NASA and companies around the world come to Bay Cast for their highly specialized needs. And bear in mind, Scott is not an engineer. He holds

degrees in biology and business, but took over Bay Cast with almost zero knowledge of the business or the complex and delicate engineering behind precision casting.

2. *A Sense of Adventure.* I'm told that at the writing of this book, Scott is on another scuba diving adventure in the Cayman Islands. He's over eighty years old now. He remains physically vigorous, in spite of his recent bout with myasthenia gravis. No one can truly be an adventurer without having that kind of bias toward action and a passion for doing, especially new things.

3. *Integrity.* Some people you can just trust. Scott is one of them. Integrity produces people's trust in you, and once trust is broken, there is no return. The best testament to Scott's ability to garner trust doesn't come from friends like me, but from the people who work for him. The loyalty his people at Bay Cast feel for him tells it all. Imagine, this guy has little or no knowledge of your foundry business, which is going to be shut down, but he says stick with me and let's finish the work on hand. The team wins: he takes over the company and dramatically grows the business thereafter. Somehow, the people on the production floor trusted him to turn the business around, with no certainty that they would even get paid. But Scott kept it alive, and the only

reason he could do that was because the people who worked there trusted him, knowing him to not only be a smart guy but a man of his word.

4. *Being a Measured Risk-Taker.* Every time an astronaut sets foot in a spacecraft, a rocket, or climbs into a space suit, he or she is taking a life-and-death risk. The Space Shuttle had a total of 136 missions, with two ending in the death of the entire crew. That's a 1.5 percent fatal failure rate, but that's the space business. You can minimize the risk by staying calm, looking at the data, and methodically developing and executing the plan when things go wrong. That's what we do as astronauts, and in this respect, Scott also has this ability: staying calm amidst chaos. I'm confident that he could have passed astronaut training. Astronauts train and train for every possible contingency, for the million-to-one critical failure scenarios, and then train some more. We are deliberately put through everything that could possibly go wrong and are carefully watched for how we react to determine our ability to have a calm demeanor in life-and-death situations. Case in point: the fire that broke out on Mir when I was staying there was about as close to a life-and-death situation as I ever want to get. But there are also non-lethal contingencies. During a spacewalk from the Russian space station Mir, while at the end of a pole, I lost sight of the space

station and had the feeling of falling at great speed. My eyes, brain, inner ear, guts—all the things we use to orient ourselves—were all misfiring at the same time, but having the ability to remain calm and focused and to talk yourself back into reorientation is a critical skill. I've been an astronaut in space and a scuba diver under the water, and I can tell you, anyone who routinely dives in environments as different as the murky ice-cold waters of Lake Superior to the fast-current warm clear waters of the Caribbean, like Scott has, has the skills.

5. *Serving the Greater Good.* Astronauts don't take risks simply for the joyride. They are motivated by service to country and science—science that will ultimately help people and the planet. Scott has served on a number of boards and foundations over the years. He had me do a commencement speech at Northern Michigan University and that's when I saw the great things he was doing to help improve people's lives. He cares. He has the mindset for sharing the good fortune he's received in life and gifting it to others who aren't as fortunate or may be struggling for resources. Take the restaurant, for example: starting a restaurant way up there in the UP was as much about preserving a landmark as it was providing a source of income to the folks there. And saving a landmark Lake Superior lighthouse

for future generations to learn from and enjoy is another example.

6. *An Astronaut's View of the Planet.* It is pretty universally well known that circling the earth every ninety minutes and seeing sixteen sunrises and sunsets every day you are in orbit changes your perspective. You feel the vastness of the universe when you're up there and realize all of humanity is down below you on that big blue ball. You soon realize that we must do right by our planet. Scott has that view and ensures that he is taking care of his special piece of the earth, King Lake. He's what I call a "realistic environmentalist," with a mindset that goes, "It's okay to cut down trees, as long as you're also planting them."

7. *Personality.* The alchemy of identifying and building great astronauts includes a multitude of factors, as I've mentioned above, but on top of all that, in addition to the intellectual hard skills such as being good at math or physics, the nature of one's overall personality is make or break. The best are quiet and thoughtful people who listen and reflect on what other people are saying. They are willing to work on problems as a team, together with others, and always make their case on the merits of their arguments, passionately make counterpoints based in logic, and never make it personal or take it personally. And again, this is precisely Scott's nature.

In conclusion, Scott is just someone you want to be around, a man of integrity and conviction whom you can trust to get things done, and done right. And, I'm so glad this book is being written about him because he certainly does have what we in astronaut circles call "The Right Stuff."

Chapter 11
The Adventurer
Larry Elliott

Larry Elliott is a retired television journalist who spent his forty-three-year career delivering the news to eastern Michigan. He spent much of that time as a news anchor but has always loved just grabbing a TV camera and using it to tell his own unique stories. Larry has received three Michigan Emmy Awards as well as numerous other professional awards for his work. He also spent the last twenty-five years of his career as news technical manager, taking care of the newsroom's computer systems in addition to his anchor and reporting duties. He's also an avid scuba diver, and during his TV career, he spent more than a decade as a search and rescue diver for the Genesee County Sheriff's Department in Flint, Michigan. At times he was called out in the middle of his workday to put on a dry suit over his dress shirt and suit pants to go search for a drowning victim. This unconventional life brought him together with Scott Holman for some interesting adventures.

* * *

SITTING 535 FEET DOWN ON THE BOTTOM OF LAKE Superior in the Royal Canadian Navy's small five-person submarine, SDL-1, I'm looking through the viewport at the shipwrecked SS *Edmund Fitzgerald*. It's 1995 and it's my third expedition to the wreck site with the Great Lakes Shipwreck Museum, this one to recover the ship's bell. Little do I know how my love for adventure will be growing, all because of one person among those supporting the bell recovery. I didn't know Scott Holman at the time, but that was about to change.

Diving since 1975, underwater exploration fascinated me since I was a kid growing up in Michigan. That was the same year I started my career in television news at a brand-new small station in Alpena. The Lake Huron shipwrecks off the coast of Alpena gave me lots to explore in my early days of diving, and my interest only grew. In 1980 I was hired by the ABC affiliate WJRT in Flint. I'd spend the rest of my career there as a news anchor and reporter. They sent me around the world to do stories with local connections, including five trips to Japan and others to Central America, Sweden, and the British West Indies. Other reports had me on a nine-hour mission aboard a US Air Force B-52 bomber, a KC-135 refueling jet where I flew the fuel line to connect to a B-52 at thirty thousand feet over Minnesota, as well as reports aboard various World War II warbirds, and even a short opportunity to pilot a Goodyear Blimp. Again, the adventure thing. Station ABC12 also gave me the freedom to report on some of my diving adventures. That led me to the Great Lakes

Shipwreck Museum on Lake Superior's Whitefish Point, where I served for twenty years on the board of directors.

I first met Scott shortly after the museum's 1995 bell recovery expedition. Another board member had convinced Scott to financially support the project and we went to his company, Bay Cast, to present him with a framed poster of the *Fitzgerald* wreck site. The poster had been taken to the site aboard the sub and was signed by members of the expedition. Over the next year or so, we got Scott interested in the museum and he joined the board of directors. Since he and I lived near each other, we often traveled together to board meetings and became good friends.

Scott likes to share his "sandbox" and an invitation to join him for diving at his place on Grand Cayman Island grew our friendship to include our families. On our first dive, I realized Scott and I have a similar level of diving skills, giving us both a great deal of comfort as dive buddies. He does have a little prankster in him, evidenced on a dive to Stingray City where he brought along a little plastic storage bag full of calamari juice and some pieces of squid. He'd cut off a corner of it, squeezing the juice into the water to bring the stingrays up close and personal. Funny (sort of) for a stingray novice like me.

We had lots of chances to talk on the boat during our diving excursions on Grand Cayman. I started to see Scott's depth as well as his "outside-the-box" approach, ranging from business to world affairs to adventure. While leaving one of our dive sites, we all forgot to bring in the underwater scooter I had clipped to a line hanging from the boat. As we took off, the scooter popped off the line and it was gone. Since we were in only about thirty feet of very clear water, Scott came up with the idea to put some of my underwater search and rescue experience to use. He started towing me slowly behind the boat, following the GPS course we were on when we lost the scooter. After about ten minutes, there it was on the bottom! He called out to me to just free dive down to get it. Now I'd been a diver for a long time but was never as great at free diving as Scott. I gave it a couple of tries without success. So Scott jumped in the water and swam to the bottom. He was gasping a bit when he came back up with the scooter. It seems I had followed procedures and locked the propeller trigger on the scooter when I'd clipped it to the line. He was counting on grabbing the scooter on the bottom and immediately using it to propel him to the surface.

Free diving on the USS Kittiwake, *Grand Cayman*

Fiddling with the lock cost him a few extra seconds. It made for a good after-dive story, and we had some laughs over it. The funny thing is, in all of our diving together, the competitiveness of each of us comes out in every dive. As we get out of our gear on the boat after every dive, the big question always comes up: "Okay, so how much air do you have left?" I have yet to use less air than Scott. I also admire the fact that he is a stickler for doing no damage to the coral reefs during our dives. He always stressed using care to not bump the coral with our fins or drag hoses or dive gauges through it.

Scott combines adventure with caring about the history of Northern Michigan. I was blown away by what he accomplished after buying the abandoned Granite Island Lighthouse. Since the lighthouse sits on a two-and-a-half-acre mound of granite twelve miles out into Lake Superior off Marquette, it can be a brutal and unforgiving environment with its sudden storms and monstrous waves. But despite huge holes left in the roof during its years of abandonment, and a rotting interior, he figured out how to restore it and found the people willing to do it. His passions are contagious.

One winter while I was at his hunting camp at King Lake, Scott needed to get out to Granite Island to finish the winter shutdown. The problem was it had been blowing like crazy on the lake for days, making it too dangerous to take out a boat. On New Year's Day the wind let up, and we had to break through some thin ice to get the boat out of the Marquette Harbor and head to the island. Most anybody who knows Lake Superior would think someone taking a thirty-foot boat on the lake on New Year's Day would be certifiable. But we pulled it off and got the dock in to avoid winter ice and storm damage and buttoned up the rest of the island for winter.

Scott has turned Granite Island into a treasure for the area, benefitting thousands of those who live nearby. His outside-the-box thinking has turned the island into a relay station, in collaboration with his alma mater, Northern Michigan University, to bring high-speed internet to areas of the Upper Peninsula previously unreached. NASA also uses the island for its Global Monitoring Laboratory to improve understanding of the earth's energy budget. One summer evening while the Shipwreck Museum Board of Directors were spending the night, we walked out on the deck around midnight and saw the most spectacular display of Northern Lights I've ever seen.

In 2004, several weeks after the Category 5 hurricane Ivan hit the Cayman Islands, Scott invited me on my next adventure with him. He was already on the island organizing repairs to his condo complex and helped me to be the first journalist on the island since the hurricane. At the time, the government was severely limiting who was allowed on the island. I packed up my TV camera, convinced the Cayman government I had a place to stay at one of Scott's undamaged condos, and headed out to do reports on the damage left behind and Scott's efforts to help some island residents who'd lost everything in the hurricane. He managed to arrange for one of very few available rental cars left running and we set out to start documenting the damage. On one trip around the island, we were out of the car shooting video when a Cayman government car slowed down, then turned around and went by again. It was somewhat a permission/forgiveness situation for me to be there shooting video, so we quickly decided wisdom was telling us to pack up and move to our next area of damage. Later that day, as we were running low on gas, we found one of a few operating gas stations on the island. As we started filling the car, we suddenly noticed gasoline spreading across the ground under the car. It turns out that people desperate for gas had reached under the car and cut the filler hose going to the gas tank so they could siphon gas to their own can. We ended up with no fire or explosion and enough gas to continue our travels.

Scott is one who loves to surprise his friends. One morning he called, asking if my wife and I had plans for the evening. He asked us and a couple of other friends to meet him at the airport that afternoon but wouldn't tell us where we were going. He suggested we bring our passports. He flew us all to Niagara Falls, Ontario. After visiting the falls, we crossed the border into the US and gathered at the Skylon Tower's revolving dining room overlooking the falls for dinner to celebrate his birthday.

Other adventures over the years include building bridges

at his Upper Peninsula hunting camp at King Lake. We built new roads by loading and driving dump trucks full of gravel, then dumping it so he could spread it out with his bulldozer. Scott also took us exploring in nearby ice caves in the middle of August. One winter I dropped everything to fly to Marquette with his pilot to help dig him out after he got snowed in at King Lake.

I believe what has intrigued Scott and me about each other during our history as adventurers is the fact that both of us tend to not approach life in conventional ways. My wife, Deb, identified it one day when she gave me a new nickname. She called me "Zag" because she realized that while everybody else is doing a zig, I'm doing a zag. I think Scott is a lot like that. I once spoke to a group of middle school students at their graduation from the DARE program [Drug Abuse Resistance Education]. During my talk, I shared the excitement of my experiences exploring the shipwreck of the SS *Edmund Fitzgerald*. I told them you don't need drugs to get high, because it's so much more fun to get high on life! Through our friendship, Scott and I have done a lot of that.

Chapter 12
Mt. Shasta
Elizabeth Wahlstrom

I t was early 2018. The harsh winter had damaged the roof of the historic Mt. Shasta Lodge Restaurant in Michigamme, Michigan, threatening to collapse it. It had been closed for business for some time. My husband, CEC [certified executive chef] Tom Wahlstrom, and I had spent our careers in the hospitality industry, owning and operating many different types of restaurants over the years as a team. He ran the back of the house, and I ran the front of the house. We have a successful catering company as well, specializing in destination weddings and celebrity golf outings. We also have a consulting business where we help entrepreneurs open and create the structure for new restaurants, from décor and manuals, to training and hiring, to creating a social media platform—all aspects of new business, and we run it until the individuals hired are ready to take over.

The phone call came from Scott Holman, requesting our assistance in the reopening of Mt. Shasta Lodge. Our decision was easy. Working for and with Scott was an honor. A brilliant businessman of many years in so many different aspects of life, his success speaks for itself in the multitude of projects he has inspired, created, and participated in.

We began immediately. Scott and I were working together to empty the entire building carefully to hopefully preserve anything we found of a historic nature. Meanwhile, Scott had hired the best in the business for the reconstruction of the building, bringing it back to as close to its original state as possible. One afternoon he brought me what looked like a large empty cardboard box from the basement, from which he produced several original black-and-white eleven-by-fourteen-inch photos from the set and cast of the movie *The Anatomy of a Murder*. One of the pictures was of his own cousin who was an extra in a music number.

He shared with me the history of his love and passion for the restaurant and why it all meant so much to him to bring it back for the community, both locals and tourists alike. While weekending at their cabin on Lake Michigamme, he and his father dined at Mt. Shasta regularly. A major scene of the movie was filmed there when he was a boy, and he was fortunate to have met and gotten autographs of all the cast members, including Duke Ellington, Jimmy Stewart, and Lee Remick, to name a few. His father, whom he adored and admired, gave him the paperback book of the movie, a number one best seller in America, and the signatures he got are in his copy.

After several months of hard work and relentless commitment, Mt. Shasta Lodge Restaurant reopened late that summer. The walls are adorned with the photographs of the movie he had restored and framed. The movie runs on a continual loop on the TVs at the bar and in the restaurant. The video is displayed for sale, as well as copies of his own copy of the book for sale and the enjoyment of his guests.

Not long after the introduction of the new Mt. Shasta Lodge Restaurant, Covid happened. And like so many other businesses and people, Mt. Shasta took a devastating blow. Everything shut down. Severe rules and restrictions began for any chance of reopening. Again, restructuring began. And then the worst possible news happened: Scott was battling Covid in an ICU downstate. His family was rallying faithfully to bring him home healthy and safely. He emerged after battling for several days, a bearded man, ready to get back to business as usual. I think one of the most important conversations we had around that time was when he showed me that he carried in his pocket a hand-written thank-you note from his grandson. A tear fell from his eye as he read it to me. He felt lucky to have survived that horrific pandemic.

Soon after reopening from the closure due to Covid, we received a call from Maurice Ball. His family members were the original owners of Mt. Shasta Restaurant Lodge. He grew up in the house connected to the restaurant. They had planned a reunion for his family at the restaurant pre-Covid; however, they lost family members during that tragic time but decided to celebrate their lives and heritage anyway. We hosted one hundred members of the Ball family at Mt. Shasta, closing the restaurant to the public for their celebration, and what a celebration it was. The stories of the history of this special place were unique.

I am grateful for the many opportunities I have had to get to know Scott better with every meeting and conversation. I have long known his background, his adventures, his successes, and his business brilliance. The Scott Holman I have come to know is a man of great love for his family; a man who sacrifices his time to better his community; a generous man who gives whatever is needed to help those who maybe cannot otherwise help themselves. He is a shining example to others, a dear loyal friend, a devoted husband, father, and grandfather.

Epilogue

As a doctor of philosophy, I have focused the last thirty-five years of my life on optimal performance coaching for professional athletes, entrepreneurs, entertainers, and a host of others from all walks of life. Over the years, I have witnessed coaches, movie producers, and others referring to one of their players, on whatever field of play, as having that special something that we commonly refer to as "It." As a result of this, I became very interested in what "It" is.

Some argue that we are born with "It." Others postulate that "It" is a function of how we are raised. This nature-nurture debate is ongoing and there are instances where arguments on both sides make some sense. My belief is that being assessed by others as having the "It Factor" is really an outward expression of one's inside thoughts. If this is true, then each of us has the power to unleash our "It Factor" in ways that will cause others to assess us as having that special "It-Factor" quality.

The bottom line for me is that receiving an "It Factor" assessment from others is the result of an outward expression of inward internal dialogue—the self-talk conversation that paints a desired picture and triggers positive emotions and responses from those around us.

Cognitive Psychology and Neuroscience

In this book's foreword, I introduced the concept of controlled internal dialogue as being an "It Factor" for successful people. A real-world example of this internal self-talk is one person who asks, "What if this happens?" whereas another might say, "So what if this happens?" and the outcomes that each of these mindsets bring. The nature of one's positive internal dialogue is truly the secret sauce to success in life, family, and career. Here, with Scott Holman's life story fresh in our minds, we'll examine three dimensions that arise from those high-performance thought processes— the controlled internal dialogue that guided Scott through his personal and professional life.

- Those who possess charm and personal magnetism

This is a personal aura that commands attention when one enters a room. It's not just about looks but also about how one carries oneself—the way one walks, talks, and interacts with others. More than any other factor, we are most tempted to assume that this is inborn, that some people have just got "It," and some people don't. True, not everyone can sculpt like Michelangelo, sing like Luciano Pavarotti, or play basketball like Michael Jordon in his prime. But those are specific talents, whereas being more charming and magnetic can be learned, no matter your physical attributes. In Scott's case, he unabashedly points to his Jaycees participation as "a very important part of my leadership development [that] . . . taught me how to run meetings and give interesting and well-prepared speeches." In short, Scott worked at it throughout his thirties, spending precious time between work and family to consciously and deliberately learn how to run civic and business organizations.

- Those who are excellent communicators

These people listen attentively, articulate their thoughts eloquently, and engage others (seemingly) effortlessly. Their words inspire, motivate, and influence those around them. Throughout this book we've heard others describe Scott as a two-way conversationalist, a deliberate listener, and a thoughtful person who listens and reflects on what other people are saying. On the outbound side of the equation, it seems there was no venue left unused by Scott for sharing his knowledge and experience for the benefit of others—whether it was volunteering to teach communists free enterprise, coaching chamber members to focus on fulfilling their organization's mission, or being the proverbial salesman who could sell refrigerators to Eskimos.

Listening and speaking are also learned skills that one can

acquire through deliberate effort and practice. Mastering listening can be as simple as convincing yourself that listening isn't just time spent waiting to say what you want. As for speaking, there are any number of organizations that have a mission to help people learn to be good speakers—publicly or one-on-one. For example, Toastmasters International describes itself as "an educational organization that operates clubs worldwide for the purpose of helping people develop communication, public speaking, and leadership skills."

Hugh Downs, once a household name, was a prominent radio and television broadcaster and announcer, news anchor, and information personality from the 1950s to the 1990s. During a post-career interview, Downs was asked to reflect on his career. He volunteered that in the beginning, he was petrified with stage fright. He explained that during his first radio show broadcasts, he was so nervous that his script was shaking in his hands, so he would hold the script and also grip his suit lapels so he could stop the script from shaking to be able to read what was written. When asked if he still suffers from stage fright, Downs replied with a smile, "Well, after fifty years of doing this, no, I don't get nervous anymore."

If someone wants to be a better communicator, the tools are all around them. They only need to pick them up and make the effort.

- Those who remain genuine and authentic

The key to success is sincerity. If you can fake that, you've got it made.

— George Burns, vaudeville, radio,
movie, and television entertainer

This quote is humorous and relevant for the world of entertainment, where people are paid to play fictional characters, but it is important not to confuse the entertainment world with the real world, where the opposite is true: Those who succeed in the long run don't put on a facade or try to be someone they're not. They are comfortable in their own skin and not afraid to show vulnerability. Sincerity in human relationships manifests as the perceived personality traits of genuineness and authenticity.

These things require more than just professional training. There are no "Jaycees" or "Toastmasters" where you can develop, practice, and hone your genuineness and authenticity skills. Those things come from the heart. But there is hope and it comes from the core philosophy of Aristotle. Aristotle's basic insight is that if you want to become something, act as if that is what you already are. If you want to become instinctively brave, act as the brave one does. Then it will become natural to you.[1] Say and do things that sincere, genuine, and authentic people do, consistently and long enough, and it will become your nature.

JASON JENNINGS[2], A PROLIFIC AUTHOR AND AUTHORITY on business leadership, innovation, and growth, once told Scott Holman, "I've been watching your career, and you are a

Renaissance man." Scott was surprised by this direct and personal assessment from someone of Jennings's intellectual stature. At first, he wasn't sure what Jennings intended with his comment, but eventually concluded it was a generous compliment. Scott shares his reflections on the encounter: "To my understanding, a Renaissance man is someone who has a collection of life experiences that is so profound and varied that you are able to draw on it to move ahead with whatever you're currently working on." This does indeed describe Scott Holman to a T.

Notes

1. The SISU Yooper Innovator

1. James Kurtti, "Finns in Michigan," Finland Abroad, January 24, 2018. https://finlandabroad.fi/web/usa/finns-in-michigan/.

2. The Imprint Years

1. Rudolf Berlin, originator of the term dyslexia. Rudolph Wagner, Annals of Dyslexia (1973), 57–63.

8. Preserving Michigan's UP Treasures

1. WPA, or Works Progress Administration, was a government-funded work project program created by the Franklin D. Roosevelt administration in 1935, designed to alleviate unemployment during the Great Depression of the 1930s.

9. PERMA

1. Martin Seligman, "PERMA and the Building Blocks of Well-Being," The Journal of Positive Psychology, February 16, 2018. https://doi.org/10.1080/17439760.2018.1437466/.

10. The Right Stuff

1. John Uri, "25 Years Ago: Fire Aboard Space Station Mir," NASA website, February 23, 2022. https://www.nasa.gov/history/25-years-ago-fire-aboard-space-station-mir/.
2. Jerry M. Linenger, *Off the Planet: Surviving Five Perilous Months Aboard the Space Station MIR* (McGraw-Hill, 2000).

   Linenger, *Letters from MIR: An Astronaut's Letters to His Son* (McGraw-Hill, 2002).

Epilogue

1. Tamar Gendler, "Lecture 9 - Virtue and Habit I" (class lecture, PHIL 181: Philosophy and the Science of Human Nature, Open Yale Courses, Yale University, New Haven, CT). https://oyc.yale.edu/philoso phy/phil-181/lecture-9/.
2. Tyler J. Markle, "Remembering Jason Jennings," Upper Michigan Resource, May 27, 2020. https://www.uppermichiganssource.com/content/news/Remembering-Jason-Jennings-world-renowned-author-businessman-and-Yooper-570808601.html/.

Made in the USA
Las Vegas, NV
24 September 2024

3f86c319-99b6-41c3-8272-eb132d29d6abR01